gardening with
INDIGENOUS TREES

DAVID & SALLY JOHNSON

First published in 2002 by Struik Publishers
(a division of New Holland Publishing (South Africa) (Pty) Ltd)
London • Cape Town • Sydney • Auckland
New Holland Publishing is a member of the Johnnic Publishing Group

Garfield House
86-88 Edgware Road
W2 2EA London
United Kingdom
www.newhollandpublishers.com

80 McKenzie Street
Cape Town
8001
South Africa
www.struik.co.za

14 Aquatic Drive
Frenchs Forest, NSW 2086
Australia

218 Lake Road
Northcote, Auckland
New Zealand

ISBN 1 86872 775 0

1 3 5 7 9 10 8 6 4 2

Publishing manager: Annlerie van Rooyen
Managing editor: Lesley Hay-Whitton
Design director: Janice Evans
Concept design: Alison Day
Designer: Illana Fridkin
Editor: Monique Whitaker
Proofreader: Inge du Plessis
Indexer: Mary Lennox

Copyright © 2002 in published edition: Struik Publishers
Copyright © 2002 in text: David & Sally Johnson
Copyright © 2002 in photographs: David Johnson, with the following exceptions:
Peter Pickford/Struik Image Library (SIL), page 6 (top); Nigel J. Dennis/SIL, 8 (all); and Geoff R. Nichols,
16 (left), 27 (right), 28 (both), 37 (right), 39 (bottom left), 40 (left), 48 (right), 57 (left), 62 (right), 67 (left), 70 (both),
76 (left), 79 (bottom right), 80 (right), 85 (top left), 90 (top left), 98 (right), 104 (right), 106 (right), 109 (left)

Front cover: *Bridelia micrantha* (red) and *Celtis africana* (green)
Back cover: *Calpurnia aurea* (left), *Xymalos monospora* (middle), *Pappea capensis* (right)
Title page: *Dovyalis longispina*

Reproduction by Hirt & Carter Cape (Pty) Ltd
Printed by Craft Print Pte Ltd

All rights reserved. No part of this publication may be reproduced, stored in a retrieval system
or transmitted, in any form or by any means, electronic, mechanical, photocopying or otherwise,
without the prior written permission of the publishers and copyright holders.

Log on to our photographic website www.imagesofafrica.co.za for an African experience.

CONTENTS

INTRODUCTION	4
GARDENING WITH INDIGENOUS TREES	4
Planning your garden	4
Wind and frost	4
Treating seeds	5
Planting seeds	5
Cuttings	6
Preparing a hole and planting	6
Post-planting care	7
Using chemicals	7
CREATING A BIRD, BAT AND BUTTERFLY GARDEN	7
Structuring your garden	7
Natural food supply	7
Good insect trees	7
Good flowering trees for birds	8
Fruit trees popular with birds	8
Good nesting trees	8
Encouraging bats	8
Encouraging butterflies	8
HOW TO USE THIS BOOK	9
KEY TO SYMBOLS	9
INDIGENOUS TREES	10
INDEX	110
GLOSSARY	112
KEY TO SYMBOLS	112

INTRODUCTION

While not all trees are large, some of them are the largest living things that have ever existed. Their size, especially their height, adds an extra dimension to the landscape, and creates a strong impact in any garden. Trees have another unique quality – their great age. The lineage began 380 million years ago, with the appearance of the ancestors of modern tree-ferns and cycads.

Gardening with indigenous trees

Wholly indigenous gardens are not as modern a concept as is generally supposed. The Aztec king Montezuma I, an ancestor of the last and famous king of that name, created a garden entirely from wild plants surrounding his palace in the 15th century.

Today, throughout the world, but especially in South Africa, indigenous trees are taking centre stage. There is pride and interest in local flora. It adds diversity to the garden, which becomes a veritable storehouse of memorable veld experiences. Many of the country's indigenous plants have traditional uses, or feature in history and folklore.

- **Indigenous to where?** Indigenous plants often seem to get bad publicity, though, for the indigenous concept is very often misunderstood or misapplied. Indigenous means homegrown, local; occurring naturally, without artificial assistance, in a defined place. This last phrase is important, for everything is indigenous somewhere. Botanically speaking, South Africa really is a world in one country, and thus the definition 'indigenous to South Africa' is too wide.

This explains some disappointing failures in growing 'indigenous' plants. Not all are tough; some plants grow naturally in very small areas and may have specialised requirements. The key to success in the garden, just as with growing exotic trees, is to concentrate upon species suited to local climate and habitat. However, this does not mean using only strictly local species. Many indigenous plants are versatile and grow well almost anywhere. Every entry in this book gives details of the type of climate and conditions under which that particular tree will do well, and the list of symbols provided for each tree gives you this information at a glance.

Planning your garden

While a new bare plot may look daunting, it is the best proposition for an inventive enthusiast. By contrast, a mature, gracious garden usually contains too many big, thirsty, shady, alien trees to allow much scope for developing an indigenous garden. It is best to remove all or most of these as soon as possible. You may be tempted to grow choice replacements in between them for a year or so before felling, but this does not really work. The newcomers struggle in the dim light, and any water or compost given to them is devoured by their rivals. Several years' painful growth can also be lost when the alien is felled, as it may well land on top of the new tree.

- **Maximise sunlight** Shade is the biggest single obstacle to tree cultivation. The very reason trees evolved in the first place was purely to avoid shade. Why else the investment in a huge woody trunk that contributes nothing directly to the tree's growth, nor to reproduction? So, almost by definition, all trees like full sun. This is usually true even of trees that are typically found in the shade in the wild. These species are too small to compete for full light in a forest, but are fire-sensitive and, therefore, cannot survive alone in an open habitat. Trees like this come into their own in cultivation.
- **How big will my tree get?** Knowledge of growth rates and mature sizes is essential for successful gardening. Sizes quoted in the text are height times spread. At least one fast-growing tree is usually needed in the primary plan, if only to see instant results. Note that growth details cited in the species accounts must obviously be approximate, and will vary according to local conditions. Cool or dry climates usually inhibit growth, and a plant in full sun may grow at 10 times the speed of a shaded neighbour. Growth rates also vary with the age of the plant. Generally short-lived species grow at their maximum rate in the first year, slowing thereafter. Long-lived species tend to grow at a rate proportional to their size in their early career, so that growth rate may be slow initially, but will accelerate up to middle age.

Wind and frost

The way in which you plant your trees is not the only factor that will determine how well they grow – frost and wind can also be significant. Where they are likely to have an impact, you can modify their effects by planting the appropriate tough sheltering trees first. The rest of your garden can then develop in relative comfort a year or two later.

- **Dealing with frost** The incidence of frost is strongly influenced by local topography and other conditions. North-facing slopes and hill-tops always receive less frost than adjacent south-facing slopes and valley bottoms. Similarly, hilly, irregular country is less affected by cold than flat open spaces, where wind aggravates the effect of frost. Thick vegetation provides some shelter against frost. These factors are very often overlooked when new gardens are planned in frosty areas. Just because a plant thrives in the surrounding bush, it will not necessarily survive in a bare garden, which is often a hostile environment, as it provides little of the shelter trees typically find in the wild.
- **Wind and soil quality** Wind is generally strongest at the coast. Prevailing winds are supplemented daily

TOP: *Acacia nigrescens*
MIDDLE: *Galpinia transvaalica*
ABOVE: *Ochna arborea*

by air currents resulting from the different temperatures of land and sea. Very few plants enjoy wind, since it causes structural damage and accelerates water loss, both from the plant and the soil. Wind also has the ability to shift loose sand, thereby sorting dune sand by grain size. The coarsest grains form the dunes nearest the sea, with progressively finer material being blown inland. Lime-rich shell fragments are lighter than sand, so these too are blown inland, adding lime to the soil there. This leaves the first dunes stripped of lime, and consequently they become acid. The result is that the first dunes offer particularly hostile prospects, virtually ruling out any conventional gardening near a beach.

- **Open Space** Whatever the planting area available, an essential feature in the layout is open space. Natural habitats all have clearings, and it is from such vantage points that everything can best be viewed. One approach is to pack the garden boundaries with trees, since this creates privacy and maximises open space. The ideal is to use only small trees on the northern boundary, to allow full sunlight in, and to place bigger trees on the southern boundary. The rest are best put in the kind of groupings found in the wild, especially in a large garden. Here, nature points the way – a bush clump often contains only one large tree, with any number of smaller trees and shrubs, usually with more than one of the same species, crammed in underneath. Copy that. There is much to be said for combining plants from the same wild environment, especially if you are attempting to grow the trees outside their natural climate or soil type. Any special care, for example extra water or special soil treatment, can then be concentrated where it is needed.

Treating seeds

Nearly all indigenous trees are best grown from seed, and, unless otherwise stated, all seeds need much the same treatment. The seeds should normally be separated from the rest of the fruit, whether they are to be planted or stored. This is especially important in the case of soft fruits, which rapidly become mouldy, with the fungus then killing the seeds. Alternatively, the moisture retained by soft fruit may be enough to trigger germination before the seed is planted in a suitable bed.

If seed is going to be stored, it must be kept dry, as it will remain inert in this state. In the wild this enables it to survive difficult conditions for a time. Indeed, some species have a compulsory dormant period, which ensures that they germinate at the best time. Dormancy provides the seed with insurance against extinction during drought or cold. Some species display intermittent germination, meaning that not all the seeds in one batch will germinate at the same time, even when the perfect conditions are provided. The significance of this is that the seeds cannot be 'fooled' into all germinating at once by the first wetting, since the moisture provided by one brief shower may well not be enough to establish the seedling properly.

- **Plant your seed right away** All species of tree seeds are best planted right away, for their viability will always diminish with age. The seeds of some tree species are worthless after as little as just three days. Germination commences once the right combination of water, oxygen and warmth is provided. The ideal combination is not known for most indigenous plants, and germination times vary a lot. So, the trick is not to give up too soon. There are some seeds that also require light in order to germinate. This is generally true of small seeds that do not have sufficient inner food resources to sustain growth away from sunlight. They are also vulnerable to fungal attack if they are left in the shade. Larger seeds (ones roughly over 1 cm long, such as those of *Podocarpus*) are designed to germinate in partial shade, the resulting seedling remaining almost dormant until sunlight penetrates a gap in the forest canopy, causing it to spring suddenly to life. However, under nursery conditions such large seeds will germinate perfectly well given light. Even though they have their own food stores to sustain them in the shade, the extra energy from the sunlight will certainly not go amiss. Germination can sometimes be speeded up if you make sure that the seed gets the right pre-treatment. This usually involves weakening the resistance of the seed coat, either by abrasion, soaking in hot water, passage through the gut of a bird or mammal, or scorching in a fire.

- **Dealing with tough seeds** The best way of abrading seeds is to scrape them, one at a time, on sandpaper or a metal file. Hard seeds, especially larger ones, benefit from this. Such seeds also respond well to hot water treatment. To treat the seeds, put the ones that are not germinating in a basin and pour boiling water over them. Then leave them to soak for up to a day, until they swell. You can also try using wild birds – they are great natural seed processors, and their effect has been copied using the services of a tame turkey in a pen, where its droppings can easily be collected. Fire treatment too can help with tough seeds. This is best provided by piling dry grass over a heap of seeds and setting fire to it. By placing the seeds in a pile, you ensure there are some that get the optimum scorch, whether they are on the outside or the inside of the heap.

Planting seeds

Plant the fresh or treated seeds in a seed bed, at a depth equal to their own size. A seed bed contains a germinating medium of 50% finely milled pine bark, 25% sand and 25% compost. A 15-cm layer of this is adequate, if good drainage is provided by an underlying layer of coarse gravel and broken bricks. Enclose the bed with a low wall to keep out all other plants. Keep the seeds damp, but not sodden, and do not give up too quickly – several species take up to a year to germinate. The seed bed should never be in full shade – keep it under 30% shade-cloth or under glass. In warmer areas seeds can be planted at any time of the year, but avoid winter planting in colder areas. Once they have grown their first few leaves, seedlings can be potted in the same mixture used in the seed bed, or a mixture of equal parts topsoil, sand and compost. Never use just garden soil, as it cakes solid and roots are unable to develop. Moreover, it is often full of weed seeds. Hold the seedling, roots dangling, with one hand, and fill the container around it until all roots are covered. This way they are arranged in a natural position and do not get damaged. Press the potting medium down by hand so that the seedling stands upright without support. Water a little, regularly, until the plant is established. Do not plant tiny seedlings directly into the garden; they dry out too quickly, and may even not be found again among larger plants.

Cuttings

Many trees grow easily from stem or tip cuttings; these are best taken in July and August if you live in a warm area. Mid-September is better in cooler areas. Tip cuttings generally work best with soft-wooded plants. Cut a section long enough to include four nodes – a node being the section between adjoining leaves. For hardwood cuttings discard the soft terminal growth altogether; the cutting must consist of last year's, or even older, hard wood. Again, four nodes' length is ideal.

- **How to take a good cutting** A clean cut with a sharp implement is essential. Ragged cuts will fray, usually leading to rot. It is important to work fast, since cuttings rapidly dry out. Plunge fresh cuttings instantly into water or wrap them in wet newspaper, as a plant is essentially a pump, and the entry of air bubbles will block its water passage. Succulent cuttings are the exception; they do better if allowed to dry for a few days in a dry shady spot until a callus forms over the cut surface. Roots will then sprout from this. Rooting hormone can be applied to the cut end before planting; it tends to make very little difference in warmer climates, but it can improve success in cooler areas.

Cuttings sometimes root if stuck straight into the ground, but, to avoid damaging the cutting, make the hole with a blunt stick rather than with the base of the cutting. Put two nodes into the hole, leaving two sticking out. Chances are improved if they are started in river sand, especially if a mist-bed is available. In a mist-bed, which must be housed under glass to retain humidity, a pre-programmed automatic water-sprayer delivers a fine mist at frequent intervals over the cuttings. Without a mist-bed, water sparingly and often. Trim off all, or most of, the leaves on a new cutting, for without roots it cannot supply enough water to all its leaves. New cuttings like shelter; use either glass or 50% shade-cloth.

- **Cuttings from roots made easy** Root cuttings (sections of root simply cut into 20-cm sections), buried 2–3 cm deep in river sand, work best for some tree species, *Cladostemon* and *Commiphora* being good examples. Make sure you keep the sand damp, as for stem cuttings.

Whatever the type of cutting, the time to transplant it to an individual pot is when new leaves sprout. Check to see if roots are at least 2 cm long. If so, replant cuttings just as though they were seedlings, and subsequent treatment should be the same too.

Preparing a hole and planting

The ideal time to plant out is in spring, as soon as the last winter frost is safely past. This allows the longest possible time for the young tree to grow before cold weather next stops growth. Roots begin growing once the weather starts warming up; growth is retarded if the roots are cramped in a pot.

It is vital to give a tree the best possible start. It has already cost money or effort, and will give great pleasure for years to come. Moreover, if it is a rare or unusual species, it may be impossible to replace later. So do not skimp on preparing the hole. The absolute minimum size for a planting hole, in good soil, is 60 cm square; a 1-m hole is needed in poor soil. Put the topsoil in one heap, the subsoil in another. The difference between the two is usually obvious, subsoil often being coarser and stonier, or consisting of solid clay, while topsoil always has a lighter feel and contains finely fragmented leaf litter. Discard any big stones.

- **Home soil** There are a few tree species that seem to need some soil from the areas where they are found naturally, growing painfully slowly without it. They probably depend upon a vital micro-organism in the soil. The only foolproof way to ensure you've got the right soil is to take some from the base of a wild tree of the same species – taking soil from nearby areas, even if they are within the tree's overall general range, won't help. Incorporate this soil from the tree's natural range into the topsoil heap that will be used to fill the hole.

- **Drainage and filling** Test drainage by filling the hole with water. If it drains away very slowly then abandon that spot, unless you are planting a swamp-loving tree. If all is well, fill the hole, mixing the soil in a 3:1 ratio with compost or completely rotted manure. Put the topsoil in the bottom of the hole where it will be of most use. The only extra fertilizer you need is a handful each of superphosphate and 2.3.2, to be mixed into the soil already in the hole.

- **Planting the tree** Fill the hole, gently treading the mixture down, to the point where the tree – still in its container – sits in the hole at the desired height. Remove the tree for the moment. Now fill the hole with water, and allow it to drain away. Do this at least six times so that the original hole and its surrounds are completely sodden. Carefully remove the plant from its container without disturbing the ball of soil holding the roots. Replace the tree and soil ball in the hole. If it leans naturally, tilt the soil ball until the stem is vertical; this is better than staking the tree later. Then fill the rest of the hole with the soil mixture and water once more. Place a mulch around the plant, on the wet soil, to reduce evaporation.

TOP: Malachite sunbird
MIDDLE: *Cassia petersiana*
ABOVE: *Gonioma kamassi*

Post-planting care
Except in unusual circumstances, never water the tree again. However, in an emergency, leave a finely trickling hose at the tree base for several hours: never, never use a bucket or watering can. If a tree was properly watered initially, there should now be enough water beneath the tree to last for weeks, at least until the next rain. In dry weather, soil water moves upwards, so the tree's roots will always be in contact with damp soil. Moreover, a degree of drought resistance can be instilled into any plant by growing it in dry conditions. Such plants have smaller leaf cells and a thicker cuticle. So don't pamper a young tree if drought is to be a perpetual problem. If it overcomes a dry period shortly after planting, it is likely to withstand drought reliably thereafter. Subsequent superficial watering is actually counter-productive, since it encourages growth of surface roots at the expense of deeper-growing roots that secure the tree's future. Trees with surface roots are much more likely to be blown over, and will continually suffer water-stress, necessitating endless watering. If a tree droops, let it droop: if it dies, plant something more suitable for your garden's particular conditions next time.

- **Pruning properly** A word about pruning: restraint. Trees need most lower branches for balance and stability, and shed them naturally once their usefulness is past. Shaving the trunk to a top-knot, municipality-style, may speed vertical growth, but produces a lanky weakling, always likely to fall over. Staking is only a partial solution.

Using chemicals
In a word: don't. Indigenous trees never die from an attack by insects. Let a plague run its course. Chemicals kill birds, lizards and many other friendly creatures, without ever eliminating the target pest totally. Should a tree appear permanently stricken, replace it with something more suitable, rather than threaten birds and other animals.

Creating a bird, bat and butterfly garden
Nearly all gardeners enjoy the company of birds. Birds are however more than aesthetic dressing – they are great environmental indicators, their presence paying tribute to a garden's quality. In any garden there will be factors limiting bird numbers and diversity. Usually, the main problem is shortage of nest sites, followed by shortage of natural food (particularly insects) and cover. This explains why a bird table with traditional breadcrumbs is successful only to a point. The real task is to address these things that are reducing bird numbers and diversity in your garden, and to provide different habitats and resources.

Structuring your garden
The complete reconstruction of natural habitats is not essential to attracting birds and other animals. However, the general structure of your garden is very important; it must copy the irregularity of most wild habitats. The simplest 'natural' garden to create is a 'bushveld' one. This typically has open areas, with a scattering of bushes and small trees, often clumped, and a few big trees. True bushveld plants are not essential; more important is to use plants best suited to the local climate and soil conditions.

If space permits, create a 'forest' as well by planting trees close together so that the mature canopies touch. In natural forest many different trees occur together, and this species mixture creates diversity of forest structure. As well as the complete canopy there is also foliage at all heights, and a variety of resources. Use forest plants when creating a forest garden. Plants accustomed to open habitats do not grow well in shade or humidity.

- **Plant around the garden's boundaries** In nature much wildlife action occurs along habitat edges, so try to maximise the amount of 'edge' in the garden. To do this, pack plants along property boundaries and have winding strips or clumps elsewhere. This arrangement also offers the best opportunity for viewing animals.
- **A clever way to get started** A unique way to start a bird garden is to preserve a dead tree or large dead branch. A passing bird is very likely to pause there and excrete pips, the end-product of meals from surrounding veld. Within weeks new plants will sprout. Remove the undesirables, monitor the rest, and within a year or two a maintenance-free semi-natural association will develop. By definition it will attract more birds since they chose its components in the first place.

Natural food supply
With few exceptions, indigenous plants provide much more food (directly and indirectly) for local animals and insects than aliens. This is particularly true when it comes to the invertebrates required by insectivorous birds, and by nestlings of nearly all bird species. Indigenous plants, especially those occurring naturally nearby to you, have evolved over a long period together with the insects with which they coexist, and so support far more than an alien plant which has only just arrived (most within just the last 100 years or so, while these adaptations take in the region of at least 10,000 years). Indigenous plants are also more reliable fruit-producers, as their local specialised pollinating agents (that is, local insects!) are present.

Good insect trees
The smaller insects that are enjoyed by robins, shrikes and warblers tend to concentrate on white flowers with a strong smell, such as those produced by *Nuxia* and *Ziziphus*. These flowers need not be large and showy – indeed many of them are small, although produced in masses. Nor need the smell be sweet, although often it is; musty smells also attract insects. Other trees attract insects with soft fruits, especially as these become over-ripe. A heavily fruiting fig will always be full of warblers, and the clouds of fruit-flies are the target of flycatchers. Trees with edible foliage are periodically inundated with caterpillars. Small cryptically-coloured caterpillars are eaten by most birds, but the hairy types are the favourite food of orioles and cuckoos.

- **Go for loose-barked trees** When looking for a secure home insects and other invertebrates are also attracted to rough-barked trees, especially species that have loose, overlapping layers of bark. Spiders and mantises and other predatory insects lurk here, and many other species pupate under the comparative security of loose bark. Their hiding places are constantly searched by woodpeckers, barbets, woodhoopoes and black tits. Another very important source of insects, especially to thrushes and robins, is the leaf-litter layer. Always leave leaf-litter under shady trees where little or nothing is growing.

Good flowering trees for birds

Flowers that attract birds are usually red and tubular, with a pool of nectar at the very bottom. Birds stick their heads right into the tube, using their long, thin bills to reach the nectar. As they do so they collect some pollen on their heads. This is then deposited in the next flower when the bird moves on. Each flower produces a succession of florets, ensuring continuity of nectar production, so that birds return every day. The sunbirds and sugarbirds, which are attracted to these floral displays, are the most spectacular of all garden visitors. The different species of red-flowering trees all have their own flowering season, amongst them filling the calendar; so use as many as possible.

Fruit trees popular with birds

Birds also assist plant dispersal, and fleshy fruits are the reward for transporting seeds. A practical way to choose a fruiting tree is to observe which species prove attractive in the surrounding veld. Otherwise, find out whether a chosen tree will produce fruit in your area. Being 'indigenous' does not automatically guarantee that a tree will fruit, particularly if the tree is native to a distant, different climatic region where its only pollinators live.

- **Best berries** Many bird-dispersed berries are red or shiny black. Berry-bearing trees usually first fruit at two to three years, and are essential in a new garden where near-instant results are wanted. They are suitable for any omnivore. Larger soft fruits are frequently green or dull-coloured, but recognised by larger specialist frugivores such as parrots and louries that rely upon them.
- **The more variety the better** For best results plant a selection of fruiting trees, rather than concentrating on one prolific species. Choosing species that fruit at different times may induce fruit-eating birds to stay almost throughout the year. Of course this plan can still fail if only one individual of a single-sexed tree is used and it turns out to be a male (male trees do not produce fruit). If space permits, always plant two or more of any such species; otherwise play safe and use bisexual trees.

Good nesting trees

Birds will chose the type of nest site best suited to their particular needs. An average garden might be used by about 50 bird species, but only a very few will nest there. In the wild the most popular sites are dense thickets, spiny trees, tree holes, and tufty or long grass on the ground. Few conventional gardens provide these things. And domestic cats are efficient killers.

Spiny plants provide direct protection against predators. Fragile, soft-wooded species are easily excavated by hole-nesters, especially at a broken branch or an old knot-hole. Dead trees supplement this function. If necessary, you can create one by ring-barking something expendable. If your dead tree lacks nest holes give the bird a start. Drill a 4–5-cm diameter hole into the trunk to a depth of 15–20 cm. Locate the hole immediately below a large branch and aim slightly upwards so that rain cannot collect in it. Dead trees also provide shelter for all sorts of small animals, and their rotting wood acts as a useful slow-release food store for many years.

- **Make an artificial nest** Alternatively, attach a short length of soft wood, such as sisal, to a branch. Chip a small hole through the sisal's harder outside surface. Some hole-nesters prefer to custom-build their own nest, and will readily do so given this sort of encouragement. You can also buy nest boxes, which make a fair substitute for natural tree holes. A simple, light-proof box, with internal dimensions of 6–12 cm square by about twice the depth, suffices. Make sure you drill a few small drainage holes in the base. The roof must be hinged, not fixed, so that debris can be removed, if necessary, once a nesting cycle has finished. The size of the entrance hole often determines which bird uses the nest, for the biggest bird that can squeeze in will do so. Position the hole high on the side of the box. Fix the box in a conspicuous spot at least 3 m above ground level, and on the underside of a diagonal branch so that rain cannot easily enter.

Encouraging bats

Bats occur throughout South Africa, and in every habitat, so all gardens already have them whether their owners realise it or not. Several things can be done to improve conditions for bats. First, maintain an eco-friendly garden. The majority of our bats are insect-eaters, and so respond to the quantity and quality of nocturnal insect life. Second, maintain roost sites. Many bats roost in hollow trunks or branches of big dead trees, or under large pieces of loose bark – yet another reason to look after dying or dead trees. Fruit bats are best encouraged by planting their favourite fruit trees.

Encouraging butterflies

Each butterfly species lays its eggs on a favourite host plant, as emerging caterpillars are very fussy about diet. You should provide these food plants (see entries marked with the butterfly symbol) in your garden to attract butterflies. A successful hatch can reduce a tree to something resembling a string vest. However, once all the leaves are eaten, the caterpillars must die or pupate. Their precise digestion forbids them to shift to a different species of plant. After a short pause the tree will grow a complete set of new leaves. The best place to create a butterfly garden is on a ridge or hilltop. Territorial males prefer such spots where their displays can best be seen, attracting more females. Population dispersal of butterflies also tends to be via hilltops.

TOP: Cape rock thrush
MIDDLE: Peter's epauletted fruit bat
ABOVE: Grey lourie

HOW TO USE THIS BOOK

The feature below explains each aspect of the tree entries, and the symbols used in the book are explained in the key, to the right. This key is repeated on the very last page of the book, for quick-reference. Consult the glossary on the same page, page 112, for further help.

> **❶ Bolusanthus speciosus**
> **❷ Tree wistaria, Vanwykshout**
>
> **❸** ☼ ❋ ❀ ⓒ ⚒ ⚒ ❄ ☁
>
> **❹ Size:** 4–9 x 2–5 m (wild), up to 8 x 4 m (garden)
> **❺ Natural habitat:** *Bolusanthus* is found naturally in Zululand, as well as in the warmer and drier parts of the far north and east of the country.
> **❻ Growth form:** This tree grows erect and slender, with a narrow crown, although its branches sometimes droop. Older specimens develop neatly fissured bark. The flowers are mauve and pea-shaped, making a wonderful display in spring, and the leaves are a favourite of baboons. The tree is briefly deciduous in late winter.
> **❼ Propagation:** Seed.
> **❽ Uses:** This tree is widely cultivated, and thrives in a variety of environments. The ideal is a hot summer with fairly low rainfall, but it can cope with anything except a cool wet summer. It tolerates moderate frost, growing well in Johannesburg, for example. *Bolusanthus* is greatly recommended as a form and flowering tree. It is often evergreen in cultivation. Growth is fairly rapid, about 80 cm per year. The graceful shape, typical of a mature tree, appears at about four years, and first flowering follows soon afterwards.
>
> **Brachylaena discolor**
> **Coast silverleaf, Wild silver oak**
>
> ☼ ❋ ⚒ ⚒ ❄ ☁
>
> **Size:** 3–10 x 3–8 m (wild), up to 6 x 6 m (garden)
> **Natural habitat:** This species is found along the KwaZulu-Natal coast and on the eastern Escarpment. It occurs in all sorts of habitats but dominates dune forest and must be familiar to every visitor to KwaZulu-Natal's beaches.
> **Growth form:** Within the forest it may be tall and straight, but on the margins and in exposed positions it is usually a dense bush. The leaves have a dark green upper-surface, which contrasts strongly with the snow-white under-surface, the effect being accentuated by strong coastal winds. The flowers are pale cream in colour and resemble miniature thistles. The fruits are parachute-assisted, dandelion-style, and grow in fluffy heads before being blown away.
> **Propagation:** Seed or cuttings. In cultivation young plants are often multi-stemmed and pruning only partially alters this.
> **Uses:** *B. discolor* is an extremely fast-growing tree, averaging 1.5 m per year initially. This evergreen is especially useful on the coast because of its ability to survive salt-laden winds; you can grow a conventional garden, out of the wind, behind its protection. It branches low down and very strongly, so is almost impenetrable, and even one year's growth will ensure privacy. *B. discolor* grows best with high rainfall and warm summers.
>
> **❾ Pest control** The insect-friendly (no chemicals) approach to gardening will have its anxious moments. Comfort yourself with the fact that a tree stricken with caterpillars or aphids will rarely suffer a mortal blow, and the extra birds attracted will make up for the rather lacy-leafed look.

❶ The tree's newest scientific name (check the index, page 110, for old scientific names)

❷ The best-known common name(s) for the tree

❸ Symbols showing the tree's characteristics, and the conditions in which it grows best, at a glance (see the key to the right)

❹ Size the tree reaches in the wild, followed by the size it grows to in the garden

❺ The area(s) where the tree is found naturally, in the wild

❻ The way the tree typically develops – its main characteristics, such as shape, foliage, fruit and flowers

❼ How you can go about growing the tree (see the Introduction, pages 5 and 6, for details of how to propagate seed)

❽ The best uses for the tree in the garden, and the climate and conditions in which it will grow best

❾ Interesting information about indigenous trees and tips on how best to garden with them

SYMBOLS

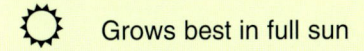

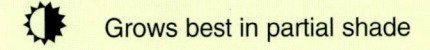

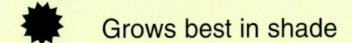

☼ Grows best in full sun

◐ Grows best in partial shade

● Grows best in shade

🌳 Deciduous tree (loses its leaves)

🌲 Evergreen tree (never loses its leaves)

❀ Flowers are an attractive feature

🍎 Fruit is an attractive feature

🦋 Attracts butterflies

🕊 Attracts birds

🦇 Attracts bats

Ⓒ Grows well in clay

⚒ Survives severe drought

⚒ Survives moderate drought

🏖 Grows well in coastal sand and withstands coastal wind

💧 Grows in waterlogged soil

❄ Survives harsh frost

❄ Survives moderate frost

❄ Survives light frost

No frost symbol: Cannot survive frost

☁ Grows best in area with high rainfall

☁ Grows best in area with moderate rainfall

☁ Grows best in area with low rainfall

Acacia burkei
Black monkey-thorn

Size: 7–10 x 8–13 m (wild), up to 8 x 10 m (garden)
Natural habitat: In the wild this species is confined to sandy soils in Zululand and the warmer parts of the northeast, and may be locally dominant. 
Growth form: Young trees are upright, but older specimens spread and have a tendency to become flat-topped. For most of the year the foliage is dense and casts a complete shade. The bark is a yellow-brown colour, similar to *A. sieberiana*, but has a different texture, being hard and fissured. Flowering and fruiting are erratic, although in a good year the bright red pods make a lovely display.
Propagation: Seed, which may be stored for several years.
Uses: *A. burkei* has not been tested much in cultivation, but it is known to thrive in Pietermaritzburg shale. *A. burkei* is a wonderful shade or specimen tree, and will grow well wherever there is slight or no frost. It makes a good bonsai. A growth rate of 50 cm per year is typical, and flowering begins at about eight years.

Acacia caffra
Common hook-thorn

Size: 3–10 x 2–8 m (wild), up to 8 x 7 m (garden)
Natural habitat: This species is found in the warmer parts of the eastern half of the country. It occurs in deciduous woodland or may grow in otherwise open grassland.
Growth form: It is an upright tree of variable size and shape, but is never flat-topped. The bark is heavily fissured and the flowers are white bottle-brushes, but the tree's finest feature is its foliage. This is a feathery, pale grey-green, and when it first appears in spring makes the freshest of contrasts with the bareness of winter. The autumn leaves turn a muted orange before being shed. Young trees have hooked thorns, but these are gradually lost with age, and mature trees may be completely thornless.
Propagation: Seed, which may be stored for several years.
Uses: *A. caffra* grows reasonably quickly in cultivation, about 70 cm per year in a warm climate. Flowering begins at five years. The canopy is not dense, and the leafless period lasts about four months, so it is not a good shade tree. It makes a craggy specimen, however, and is ideal for a wild garden.

Woodland habitat Woodland differs from forest in that the tree canopy is not continuous; indeed it may be very sparse. There is plenty of light at ground level, grass can grow, and in the dry season grass fires are likely. To survive these conditions, woodland trees have to be fire resistant, and most are deciduous and drought resistant.

Acacia galpinii
Monkey-thorn

Size: 10–25 x 12–30 m (wild), up to 13 x 16 m (garden)
Natural habitat: This, the largest of all the South African acacias, occurs in parts of the far northeast, and is much in evidence along the Limpopo River.
Growth form: Other acacias may be as tall, sometimes 20 m or more, but none has its great bulk and spread. Apart from its size and bearing, it has several other attractive features. The buds and partly open leaves are purple, and this phase in the annual cycle often coincides with the appearance of the white bottle-brush flowers. The thorns are black and contrast with the flaking, pale yellow-brown bark.
Propagation: Seed, which may be stored for several years.
Uses: *A. galpinii* makes an outstanding specimen and shade tree in the garden. It grows quickly, in a warm climate well over 1 m per year, even 2 m initially. Flowering begins at eight years. It withstands considerable frost, and is widely grown in Johannesburg, although it grows more slowly in this cold climate. It is semi-deciduous; generally the new growth in spring overlaps the last of the autumn leaves.

Acacia karroo
Sweet thorn

Size: 6–15 x 5–9 m (wild), up to 7 x 6 m (garden)
Natural habitat: *A. karroo* grows in abundance in many parts of South Africa, where it is often the most common tree.
Growth form: Size and shape vary, and some regional forms have at times been considered separate species. Inland, *A. karroo* tends to be fairly short, branching low down. On the east coast it is tall, with a clean, straight trunk. The bark is smooth and usually reddish. However, east coast trees have glossy green young branches that contrast beautifully with the large, snow-white thorns. Occasional bark wounds exude a clear, pale yellow-brown gum, which has a slightly sweet taste. Bushbabies love it. The flowers are an attractive bright yellow and appear when the tree is two to three years old. They are followed by sickle-shaped pods. Individual trees may flower three times in a single year. *A. karroo* is the host plant of several species of butterfly, notably Lycaenids and Charaxids.
Propagation: Seed, which may be stored for several years.
Uses: *A. karroo* is a marvellous garden tree since it grows in any soil in any climate. It can be used as a screen, a specimen, or a component of a bush clump, and is essential in any bird garden. Its speed of growth is rewarding – typically it grows about 1 m or more per year.

Recognising acacias South African acacias all bear thorns, mostly in pairs, sometimes in threes (or simply scattered in some scramblers), while their Australian counterparts bear no thorns at all. Once you get the hang of it, many species of acacia are recognisable from their thorns alone.

Acacia nigrescens
Knob thorn

Size: 8–15 x 8–15 m (wild), up to 10 x 10 m (garden)
Natural habitat: This acacia is widespread in Africa, but in South Africa is largely confined to the warm, dry lowlands of the east and north.
Growth form: It usually grows in single-species stands, individual trees being quite widely spaced. It tends to grow upright, and, although older specimens may spread, they never become flat-topped. The hooked thorns are retained on old growth, eventually growing into large spiny knobs. The flowers are at first rusty-pink, but white when fully open. The pink blush always peeps through the flowering display, which can be spectacular, covering the leafless tree in early spring. Baboons and kudus eat the flowers. However, flowering is erratic, and may miss out some years altogether. The leaflets are the biggest of all African acacias, and new spring growth may be bright red. This is the host plant of the butterfly *Charaxes phaeus*.
Propagation: Seed, which may be stored for several years.
Uses: *A. nigrescens* makes a particularly rewarding garden specimen, deserving a prime spot. The growth rate is about 50 cm per year in cultivation, and flowering can be expected at about 12 years. This is a good bonsai tree.

Acacia nilotica
Scented thorn, Lekkerruikpeul

Size: 3–7 x 6–14 m (wild), up to 5 x 10 m (garden)
Natural habitat: *A. nilotica* is common and widespread in dry woodlands of much of the north and east.
Growth form: Single-species stands are frequent and the tree may dominate mixed thornveld. *A. nilotica* is nearly always flat-topped, but it develops a denser crown than other flat-topped species and can cast a complete shade. Its thorns are the biggest of all South African acacia species, and curve slightly backwards at the base. Mature trees have deeply fissured bark, which is inhabited by a variety of invertebrates. The bright yellow flowers first appear at three years and are followed by beautiful beaded pods. These give the tree its common name, for they smell of granadillas when rubbed. 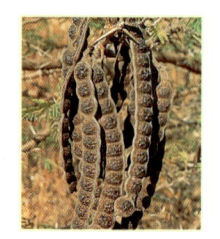
Propagation: Seed, which may be stored for several years.
Uses: *A. nilotica* is a great success in the garden provided that the climate is fairly dry and the frosts not too severe. It grows about 60 cm per year and starts spreading at two to three years. It makes a good form and a passable shade tree.

Thornveld The term 'thornveld' is given to woodland that is dominated by acacias. 'Lowveld' is woodland found at lower altitudes, especially in Limpopo Province (formerly Northern Province), and Mpumalanga and KwaZulu-Natal provinces. The term 'bush' is more general, as this denotes all sorts of woody habitats.

Acacia robusta
Splendid acacia, Enkeldoring

Size: 8–20 x 8–20 m (wild), up to 10 x 10 m (garden)
Natural habitat: *A. robusta* is fairly widespread in the eastern half of the country, often, but not always, occurring near rivers in warmer areas.
Growth form: This tree's growth is upright, and larger specimens have a rounded crown and are never flat-topped. This tree can be recognised at a distance by its dark green foliage that grows more erect than other acacias. Young trees have smooth bark that becomes deeply fissured with age. Bark wounds produce amber gum. The flowers are white and in some springs create the finest display of any flowering acacia: the blooms may be crammed together so tightly that it is impossible to fit in any more.
Propagation: Seed, which may be stored for several years.
Uses: This is an ideal garden tree, and begins flowering at six years. It grows fast in a warm climate and can tolerate almost anything except severe frost. It enjoys a high water table and will grow in a soggy spot provided that it dries out seasonally. However, it also grows well in normal, drier soil. *A. robusta* is a must for a spring garden with its fresh, almost luminous, new growth and makes a good shade tree from its fourth year onwards. Growth is rapid, at least 1 m per year.

Acacia sieberiana
Paperbark thorn

Size: 6–9 x 10–20 m (wild), up to 8 x 15 m (garden)
Natural habitat: *A. sieberiana* is the most familiar of KwaZulu-Natal's acacias, being widely distributed in the warmer parts of the midlands. It is also locally common further north.
Growth form: This tree often forms single-species stands, or may be a component of mixed thornveld. Typically, it is perfectly flat-topped. The tree produces a profusion of creamy white flowers in spring. The pods are usually heavily parasitised by insect larvae, and, since they stay on the tree for several months, they are a major attraction for birds. Birds also like the bark, which harbours many spiders, caterpillars and other invertebrates in its loose, peeling, yellow-brown layers. 
Propagation: Seed, which may be stored for several years.
Uses: *A. sieberiana* is a great success in the garden. Young trees are fast-growing, and the flat top develops when they are about four years old. Flowers first appear at about five years. The tree casts a dappled shade, allowing a lawn to grow beneath its canopy. It thrives in shale in minimal soil. Growth rate is rapid, at least 1 m per year.

Nitrogen in acacias Acacias convert inert atmospheric nitrogen into a useful soluble form. The work is actually done by *Rhizobium*, a bacterium which lives in the roots. Up to 250 kg of atmospheric nitrogen is converted per hectare per season, the equivalent of applying 2.5 tons of nitrogenous fertiliser to the soil.

Acacia tortilis
Umbrella thorn

Size: 3–7 x 8–20 m (wild), up to 5 x 12 m (garden)
Natural habitat: *A. tortilis* is widespread in the warm dry parts of the north and east.
Growth form: It is the most classically shaped of the acacias, the clean flat top drooping slightly at the edges, producing an umbrella. *A. tortilis* is especially thorny, so the canopy is almost impenetrable, and is the favourite nesting place of many birds. The flowers are white, and sometimes so profuse that the tree appears blanketed in snow. The pods twist into a tight spiral. At this stage the seeds are loose inside the pod and rattle in the wind. *A. tortilis* is often parasitised by showy mistletoes, and when these are in flower they are irresistible to sunbirds.
Propagation: Seed, which may be stored for several years.
Uses: *A. tortilis* grows easily in a dry garden, but it is essential to leave enough space for the canopy to spread, since the charm of the tree is lost if its unique shape is cramped. Growth rate is about 50 cm per year. Flowering begins at about eight years. Mistletoes can be 'planted' by placing their very sticky seed in a high fork of the tree. The parasite (which will not harm the tree) quickly 'roots', but further development under garden conditions has not so far been observed. *A. tortilis* makes a striking specimen and a fine bonsai.

Acacia xanthophloea
Fever tree

Size: 10–20 x 6–18 m (wild), up to 12 x 9 m (garden)
Natural habitat: Fever trees are common alongside rivers or around pans in Zululand and the eastern Lowveld, especially in areas prone to flooding. They can survive inundation to a depth of a metre or more for some time once established.
Growth form: The tree normally grows upright, with a straight main trunk. Only specimens that are over 30 years old will spread. The most striking feature is the bark, which is a pale, ghostly yellow, and just as attractive in the garden as it is in the wild. The foliage is fairly sparse and casts little shade. The flowers are yellow, appearing in early spring.
Propagation: Seed, which may be stored for several years.
Uses: Fever trees grow exceptionally well in cultivation, provided the summer is warm and winter frosts not too severe. Growth is rapid, often well over a metre per year. Flowers appear from the fourth year onwards, but are never as showy as the bark. The best effect in the garden can be achieved by planting a small group about 3–4 m apart, which is the typical spacing of a wild community. This encourages the trunks to grow straight, and their colour is enriched if they are placed so that they catch the setting sun.

***Acacia* flower varieties** The flowers of local acacias come in three variations: round yellow balls, round white balls and white spikes. The flowers have no true petals and are composed mainly of fluffy stamens. The pods are distinctive too, with each species having its own characteristic shape.

Adansonia digitata
Baobab

Size: 10–14 x 12–16 m (wild), up to 8 x 10 m (garden)
Natural habitat: The baobab is restricted in South Africa to the far northeast. It is always found at low altitudes in deciduous woodland, and creates much of the magic of the Lowveld.
Growth form: The enormously fat trunk is the hallmark of the mature tree, the effect being enhanced by the comparatively sparse branches and long deciduous period. However, the baobab has many other attractive features such as maple-like leaves, large white flowers with delicately crumpled petals and a big yellow stamen mass, and bulbous woody fruits with a velvet finish. Bats visit the flowers, collecting nectar from the cupped surface of the petals. All sorts of birds and other animals nest and roost in the canopy and in hollows in the trunk.
Propagation: Seed; the fresher the better.
Uses: Baobabs are not widely cultivated, partly because of the belief that they take forever to grow. While it is true that baobabs may live 2,000 years, initial growth in the garden is not slow. Given a warm summer, the growth rate is 50 cm per year. By four years the base of the trunk swells. Subsequent performance is influenced by soil quality. If clay is present the base of the trunk thickens rapidly, and a delightful miniature baobab results in as little as six years.

Albizia adianthifolia
Flatcrown

Size: 8–12 x 12–35 m (wild), up to 10 x 25 m (garden)
Natural habitat: The flatcrown occurs in evergreen forests in coastal KwaZulu-Natal and parts of the eastern Lowveld.
Growth form: The flatcrown has a clean straight trunk, with branches arcing upwards and outwards, so that the feathery foliage forms a flat, spreading layer. There is a short deciduous period if the winter is cool or dry. The flowers are white and fluffy. The pods are straw-coloured and hang from the tree in great masses during winter. Forest weavers squeeze the pods open with their feet to get at the seed parasites. The flatcrown is the host plant of three species of *Charaxes* butterfly.
Propagation: Seed, which may be stored for years. The flatcrown rapidly develops a long tap root, and does not enjoy life in a packet. It is best planted out before reaching 15 cm in height. 
Uses: It grows up to a metre per year, given a warm summer and moderate to good rainfall, and must have room to spread properly. Flowering begins at about six years. It makes a great feature and casts adequate shade, yet allows a lawn to grow beneath it. It is ideal for car parks and avenues.

Albizia This genus is very similar to *Acacia*, but never has thorns (although there are thorny exotic *Albizia* species). The flowers are also made up of stamens and are usually white hemispheres. The other look-alike, *Dichrostachys cinerea*, does not have paired thorns; instead it bears small spiny branchlets.

Androstachys johnsonii
Lebombo ironwood

Size: 8–20 x 6–14 m (wild), up to 7 x 5 m (garden)
Natural habitat: *Androstachys* is restricted to the eastern Lowveld. It is nearly always associated with rocky hill-slopes where it may be a component of mixed woodland or form single-species stands.
Growth form: This tree is upright, often slender. Young trees have all their branches at right-angles to each other. The mature tree's bark is typically coal-grey, and deeply and regularly fissured. *Androstachys* has outstanding foliage. The leaves are almost circular, and everywhere perfectly paired. There is a stark contrast between the leaves' very dark upper-surface and their snow-white, velvet under-surface. The flowers, too, are striking. Although fairly small, they have unusual spiky tubes that are yellow (male) or more-or-less white (female).
Propagation: Seed.
Uses: *Androstachys* makes an exceptional garden tree, combining as it does so many attractive features. Growth is slow, about 30 cm per year. Although semi-deciduous in the wild, the tree appears evergreen in cultivation. It needs a warm summer, and is probably frost-sensitive. Although at home in dry habitats, it grows well in high rainfall if drainage is good. It makes a stunning exhibit in a large pot.

Antidesma venosum
Tassel berry

Size: 3–7 x 3–7 m (wild), up to 5 x 5 m (garden)
Natural habitat: *Antidesma* is found along the KwaZulu-Natal coast and in the eastern Lowveld. It occurs in evergreen forest, usually at the margins, and on koppies in drier habitats.
Growth form: It is a small, chunky tree. The foliage is dense and the leaves have a waxy appearance. If rainfall is high, the tree is never leafless, but may be very briefly deciduous in dry areas. The small greenish flowers grow in catkin-like spikes that smell of honey and look like Christmas decorations on the tree. The fruits are small berries, which grow in tassels in such profusion that the tree may be covered for weeks. The berries are first green, then change to white, red, and finally black, as they ripen. All colours will be present in most tassels.
Propagation: Seed, often planted by visiting birds.
Uses: *Antidesma* makes a very nice specimen tree, and is ideal in a tall screen. Growth is rapid, about 80 cm per year, and flowering and fruiting take place at three years. This tree is essential in a bird garden. Sexes are separate, so both male and female trees are required in order to produce fruit. Since seedlings all look the same, plant three or more if space permits; spare males can be removed later. It makes a good orchid host tree.

Forest A forest is a naturally occurring community of trees in which the canopy is closed. It need not be evergreen, but usually is in South Africa. A forest is a 'climax community', unique in that it is the end-product of a series of vegetation changes, and won't change further. It is always found where water is abundant and grass fires never penetrate.

Apodytes dimidiata
White pear

Size: 4–10 x 3–9 m (wild), up to 7 x 7 m (garden)
Natural habitat: *Apodytes* is widespread throughout the wetter parts of South Africa. It occurs in almost every habitat, being most common in coastal and mist-belt forest.
Growth form: It is an upright tree, its glossy leaves forming a dense, evergreen canopy. The bark is very smooth and pale, almost white. Older trunks bear a filigree of lichens. The tree produces small, white, sweet-smelling flowers in massed, branched heads in late spring. The fruit is unusual – a flat, black berry, held in a red cup. Fruits are produced in great bunches, which cover the tree. Some crops go unnoticed, others are totally stripped by bulbuls. The rare spotted thrush picks up fallen fruits from the ground.
Propagation: Seed.
Uses: This tree is ideal for cultivation because it thrives in a wide variety of conditions, and even grows well in soggy soil. Only a hot and very dry summer, or severe frost, will defeat it. Growth is fairly rapid, about 70 cm per year. *Apodytes* makes a good shade tree, and good background foliage. It is also worth its place as a flowering and fruiting specimen. It could be used as an avenue tree where scale demands something smaller than traditional large avenue species.

Atalaya alata
Lebombo wing-nut

Size: 4–6 x 4–6 m (wild), up to 7 x 7 m (garden)
Natural habitat: This is a highly localised species, occurring in the Lebombo Mountains of Zululand and in a few nearby places. It is found on rocky slopes in dry woodland.
Growth form: It is an extremely pretty tree, typically slender. The leaves are compound with tiny leaflets, and the foliage droops gracefully. The flowers are white and small, but they are produced in large heads at branch tips, and provide a fine display in spring. The fruits form hanging bunches and closely resemble those of a sycamore or maple, with a propeller-like wing to help with wind dispersal. Young fruits are pale green, and turn bright red and finally brown when mature.
Propagation: Seed; that collected from garden plants has fewer parasites than wild seed.
Uses: *Atalaya* adapts extremely well to cultivation, a pleasant surprise in view of its narrow range and dependence upon rocky slopes in the wild. Its growth is rapid, about 80 cm per year. Flowering and fruiting begin at three years, and fruits produce viable seed even far outside the tree's natural range. It makes an acceptable shade tree in a small garden. It enjoys heat and drought, but its performance in high rainfall and frost is unknown.

Dangers of frost Frost kills plants by forming ice crystals inside their cells. These rupture the cell membranes and also concentrate the remaining sap, causing proteins vital to the plant's survival eventually to precipitate out of the sap solution. Either of these events can quickly kill the plant.

Balanites maughamii
Torchwood

Size: 8–15 x 6–12 m (wild), up to 8 x 7 m (garden)
Natural habitat: *Balanites* occurs naturally in the eastern Lowveld and northern Zululand. It is found in sand forest, and also in deciduous woodland.
Growth form: It grows upright and the trunk is invariably ribbed and fluted. Young trunks and branches are bright green, striped with white. They are very spiny, and even old trees bear spiny young shoots on the lower trunk. The crown is deep and dense. *Balanites* is semi-deciduous. The fruits are large and olive-green. They are intensely bitter, but much loved by baboons, which discard the date-like pips beneath the tree. Vultures often nest in *Balanites*.
Propagation: Seed. Because it is so large, it is best planted directly into the growing-on pot. Add plenty of rich material, such as old kraal manure, for best results when planting out.
Uses: *Balanites* makes a distinctive specimen, both in its colourful youth and in imposing adulthood. The young tree retains a green stem for several years, the characteristic fluting becomes properly developed after 10 years or so. Growth rate is slow to start with, about 30 cm per year, but accelerates to 1 m or more per year by three years. *Balanites* looks its best if given the hottest available spot.

Baphia racemosa
Natal camwood, Violet pea

Size: 3–6 x 2–5 m (wild), up to 5 x 4 m (garden)
Natural habitat: This species occurs naturally on the KwaZulu-Natal coast where it is found in evergreen forest.
Growth form: It is usually a small, well-proportioned tree. Locally common, it tends to lead a subdued existence in semi-shade. However, it prefers full sun, and in clearings or on river fringes it produces fine floral displays in mid-summer. The flowers are pea-shaped and white, with a pale orange centre. They have a strong, sweet scent. The fruit is a hard woody pod. When mature and dry the pods explode, scattering the seeds.
Propagation: Seed.
Uses: *Baphia* makes a beautiful small specimen tree in cultivation and is used as a street tree in Durban. Growth rate is about 50 cm per year. First flowering occurs at three years. *Baphia* likes high rainfall and a warm summer. However, it flowers well, even in a low-rainfall area, provided that the summer is warm, although growth is slower. It gets a little singed by moderate frost but recovers perfectly afterwards.

Sand forest Occurring in the frost-free lowlands, sand forest is confined to deep, sandy soil and is found only in northern Zululand (where it is best seen in the Mkuzi and Tembe game reserves), and the northern Kruger National Park. Sand forest is very rich in tree species, many of which occur in no other habitat.

Barringtonia racemosa
Powderpuff tree

Size: 8–10 x 6–8 m (wild), up to 7 x 6 m (garden)
Natural habitat: *Barringtonia* is found on the KwaZulu-Natal coast and rarely grows far from the sea. It always grows near water, either in swamp forest or lining the upper reaches of estuaries where there is tidal rise and fall of fresh water.
Growth form: It is a substantial tree; its branches sometimes forming neat, pagoda-like layers. The leaves are large and tropical-looking. New growth is bright red, and flushes occur throughout the year. The flowers are very beautiful, white with a pink tinge, and consist mainly of stamens, which create the powderpuff appearance. The flowers grow in long fragrant, pendant sprays. The fruits are large and fibrous, and are dispersed by water. They remain afloat for at least six months.
Propagation: Seed: keep it warm and damp.
Uses: Despite its specialised environment in the wild, *Barringtonia* adapts readily to cultivation. Growth is fast, about 1 m per year. First flowers appear at five years. *Barringtonia* makes a fine specimen tree. It does not need swampy soil, provided that the rainfall is high. However, it looks its best grouped around a large water feature, and creates the air of a tropical paradise. It must have a reasonably warm winter – absence of frost is not enough.

Bersama lucens
Glossy bersama

Size: 3–6 x 3–6 m (wild), up to 4 x 3 m (garden)
Natural habitat: *Bersama* is found in the warmer parts of the east and northeast. It occurs in evergreen forests, often on the margins, on steep slopes, and among rocks, where sunshine is more accessible.
Growth form: It is a smallish tree, with a well-developed trunk and crown. *Bersama* is one of the prettiest of all trees. The leaves are compound, brilliantly glossy and waxy pink when new, changing later to brownish-purple. The flowers are white, with long, narrow petals, held in vertical racemes, and the fruits are green capsules which split when mature, revealing brilliant red seeds. The fruits can be especially conspicuous, spangling the whole tree red.
Propagation: Seed.
Uses: This tree deserves a prime spot in the garden, if climate permits. Apart from its other merits, the fruit attracts birds. Growth rate is modest, about 40 cm per year. First flowering occurs at about six years. *Bersama* likes moderate to high rainfall and a fairly warm summer. Its bark is keenly sought-after for traditional medicine, to the point that the tree is becoming rare. Under controlled conditions this tree could be grown as a very valuable commercial crop.

Swamp and dune forest Forest composition and structure vary greatly with local conditions. On dunes next to the beach, forest has a stunted, windswept look and contains far fewer species than lowland forest. Swamp forest, which grows in soggy hollows, is also relatively species-poor, containing mainly waterlogged-soil specialists.

Bolusanthus speciosus
Tree wistaria, Vanwykshout

Size: 4–9 x 2–5 m (wild), up to 8 x 4 m (garden)
Natural habitat: *Bolusanthus* is found naturally in Zululand, as well as in the warmer and drier parts of the far north and east of the country.
Growth form: This tree grows erect and slender, with a narrow crown, although its branches sometimes droop. Older specimens develop neatly fissured bark. The flowers are mauve and pea-shaped, making a wonderful display in spring, and the leaves are a favourite of baboons. The tree is briefly deciduous in late winter. 
Propagation: Seed.
Uses: This tree is widely cultivated, and thrives in a variety of environments. The ideal is a hot summer with fairly low rainfall, but it can cope with anything except a cool wet summer. It tolerates moderate frost, growing well in Johannesburg, for example. *Bolusanthus* is greatly recommended as a form and flowering tree. It is often evergreen in cultivation. Growth is fairly rapid, about 80 cm per year. The graceful shape, typical of a mature tree, appears at about four years, and first flowering follows soon afterwards.

Brachylaena discolor
Coast silverleaf, Wild silver oak

Size: 3–10 x 3–8 m (wild), up to 6 x 6 m (garden)
Natural habitat: This species is found along the KwaZulu-Natal coast and on the eastern Escarpment. It occurs in all sorts of habitats but dominates dune forest and must be familiar to every visitor to KwaZulu-Natal's beaches.
Growth form: Within the forest it may be tall and straight, but on the margins and in exposed positions it is usually a dense bush. The leaves have a dark green upper-surface, which contrasts strongly with the snow-white under-surface, the effect being accentuated by strong coastal winds. The flowers are pale cream in colour and resemble miniature thistles. The fruits are parachute-assisted, dandelion-style, and grow in fluffy heads before being blown away.
Propagation: Seed or cuttings. In cultivation young plants are often multi-stemmed and pruning only partially alters this.
Uses: *B. discolor* is an extremely fast-growing tree, averaging 1.5 m per year initially. This evergreen is especially useful on the coast because of its ability to survive salt-laden winds; you can grow a conventional garden, out of the wind, behind its protection. It branches low down and very strongly, so is almost impenetrable, and even one year's growth will ensure privacy. *B. discolor* grows best with high rainfall and warm summers.

Pest control The insect-friendly (no chemicals) approach to gardening will have its anxious moments. Comfort yourself with the fact that a tree stricken with caterpillars or aphids will rarely suffer a mortal blow, and the extra birds attracted will make up for the rather lacy-leafed look.

Brachylaena elliptica
Bitter-leaf

Size: 4–6 x 4–6 m (wild), up to 5 x 5 m (garden)
Natural habitat: *B. elliptica* extends from the Eastern Cape to the KwaZulu-Natal Midlands. It is most common in fairly dense deciduous woodland.
Growth form: It can be upright, but is usually multi-stemmed when damaged by browsing or fire. The leaves are greyish-green above, off-white below, and the edges of the leaves are highly serrated, giving a jagged texture to the foliage. It is almost evergreen, thinning in winter. The flowers are pale cream and resemble miniature thistles. This tree's fruits are parachute-assisted, dandelion-style, and form fluffy heads. The fruits can make a spectacular display after a still, dry autumn, as they completely mask the remnants of the foliage before being blown away. 
Propagation: Seed.
Uses: *B. elliptica* grows about 1.2 m per year in cultivation, where it often flowers twice a year, the autumn display being every bit as good as that in spring. It makes a nice specimen or an adequate screen. *B. elliptica* likes moderate rainfall and a warm summer, but will survive anything except severe frost.

Breonadia microcephala
African teak, Mingerhout, Matumi

Size: 12–30 x 10–25 m (wild), up to 17 x 15 m (garden)
Natural habitat: *Breonadia* occurs naturally in the eastern Lowveld and northern Zululand. Almost invariably it is found lining permanent rivers and can be seen from Olifants Camp and many of the river bridges in the Kruger National Park.
Growth form: *Breonadia* is a tall, elegant tree. Its pleasing form is complemented by the beauty of its foliage, the leaves being narrow, pointed and brilliantly glossy. The fruits are tiny, but packed neatly into spherical rough-textured balls that stay on the tree for some time.
Propagation: Seed germination in cultivation is poor, so choose seeds of different ages from several different trees to improve prospects.
Uses: *Breonadia* makes a fine specimen and shade tree, and grows perfectly well in ordinary soil, away from water. Even in such a position fruiting begins at three years. Growth is fast, at least 1 m per year given good rainfall and a warm summer. Although it looks most appropriate next to water, *Breonadia* does not enjoy waterlogged soil. In the wild it only associates with moving water that never becomes stagnant. It can only survive the lightest frost, but tolerates an average drought.

Choose local Always choose trees that are adapted to your local conditions. Although some that are not from your area will also grow well, many won't. With local trees you are guaranteed that they are suited to your conditions, and it is much more rewarding to watch your trees growing well, not just surviving.

Bridelia micrantha
Coast goldleaf, Mitzeerie

Size: 10–18 x 10–20 m (wild), up to 13 x 14 m (garden)
Natural habitat: *Bridelia* is found on the KwaZulu-Natal coast and in the northeast of South Africa. This tree is common in lowland forest and especially so in swamp forest, yet also grows well on rocky outcrops in hot, exposed positions.
Growth form: It is a well-shaped tree with a spreading canopy. The leaves are large and glossy, with neat herringbone veins. During winter they turn a lovely range of yellow, orange and red before being shed in spring, but the new crop, which is initially metallic-red in colour, appears almost immediately. In mid-summer the tree bears berries, tightly clustered along the smaller branches. They attract fruit bats as well as birds.
Propagation: Seed, which must be fresh.
Uses: *Bridelia* grows up to 2 m per year. A good shade tree results after only three years, and first fruiting can be expected then. It provides fine background foliage in a large garden. The tree is particularly useful where waterlogging is a problem, provided that the hole in which it is to be planted does not fill with water completely. It has been used with great success in restoring damaged watercourses on over-exploited sugar-cane farms. The root system is extensive and rapidly forms a mat across the stream bottoms, halting further erosion.

Buddleja saligna
Witolienhout

Size: 4–7 x 3–5 m (wild), up to 6 x 5 m (garden)
Natural habitat: *B. saligna* is found over most of the country and grows in every climate except extreme desert. The tree is most common in dry woodland, and is often found alongside seasonal watercourses.
Growth form: It can be shrubby, but generally tends to be a small, slender tree. *B. saligna*'s branches usually grow almost vertically upwards. The leaves are long and thin, olive-green above, whitish below, giving the tree a greyish appearance at a distance. The flowers appear early in summer. They are tiny and creamy-white, forming a trumpet shape, with fine protruding stamens, which give the flowering mass a misty appearance. The flowers smell of honey, and attract butterflies and other nectar-seeking insects.
Propagation: Seed or cuttings.
Uses: This tree is ideal for a wild garden where it is best grown in a mixed bush clump. It is also pretty enough to make a specimen. Growth is quite rapid, at least 1 m per year, and flowering usually begins at two years. *B. saligna* enjoys almost any climate except a cool wet summer.

Swamp trees Adaptations to swamp life are most developed in sub-tropical forest trees. Some put up root loops above the water to collect oxygen. Others produce stilt roots on the trunk, which reach down to the ground. There they root in the soft soil and 'pull tight', guying the tree in place.

Buddleja salviifolia
Sagewood

Size: 3–10 x 3–8 m (wild), up to 7 x 7 m (garden)
Natural habitat: *B. salviifolia* is a widespread species, absent from only the arid west and the hot Lowveld. This tree is found on forest edges, in rocky grassland and alongside streams, and is common at high altitudes.
Growth form: It can be shrubby or treelike. The leaves are sage-green above, whitish below, with the texture of thick velvet. The flowers are usually creamy white, with a pale orange centre, but some trees have pale lilac flowers. The flowers are small and trumpet-like, and smell of honey. They attract butterflies and other nectar-seeking insects. This is the host plant of the butterfly *Phalanta phalantha*. 
Propagation: Seed or cuttings.
Uses: *B. salviifolia* is ideal for a wild garden, where it is best grown in a mixed bush clump or as a screen. Growth is rapid, at least 1 m per year, and flowering begins usually at two years. Because of its proven ability as a forest pioneer in cold areas it can be used on a large scale to rehabilitate degraded stream banks. *B. salviifolia* likes a cool or temperate summer with moderate to good rainfall.

Calodendrum capense
Cape chestnut

Size: 8–25 x 8–20 m (wild), up to 11 x 11 m (garden)
Natural habitat: *Calodendrum* is found in the wetter parts of the south and east, ranging from the southern Cape, through KwaZulu-Natal, and all the way along the northeastern Escarpment. It is common in evergreen forests. 
Growth form: It is a tall, well-formed, semi-deciduous tree, losing all its leaves in a cold or dry winter. It has spectacular flowers, large and pink, with long, narrow, curved petals. They cover the tree in mid-summer, making it easy to identify. The fruits are no less striking – large, woody capsules with a knobbly texture, like the edible chestnut. When mature, they split, revealing a mass of large, black seeds fitting together like a three-dimensional jigsaw puzzle. This tree is host to beautiful swallowtail butterflies, notably *Papilio demodocus*, *P. nireus* and *P. ophidicephalus.*
Propagation: Seed.
Uses: *Calodendrum* is well worth growing for its flowers or for shade. Growth rate varies. If the summers are wet and warm, 60 cm per year is likely. If the weather is cool or dry, growth will be slower. First flowering occurs at about six years.

Windbreaks If you live in a cold or windy area, plant a substantial windbreak before you try anything else. *Buddleja salviifolia* and *Brachylaena discolor* are particularly well suited to this purpose.

Calpurnia aurea
Wild laburnum

Size: 2–4 x 2–4 m (wild), up to 3 x 3 m (garden)
Natural habitat: *Calpurnia* occurs in the Eastern Cape, most of KwaZulu-Natal, and on the northeastern Escarpment. It occurs in evergreen forests, either in the understorey or at the margins, on rocky outcrops and in dry thornveld.
Growth form: It is a small, slender tree. The leaves are compound and graceful. In a dry environment with a cool autumn they turn yellow before falling. Elsewhere, *Calpurnia* is almost evergreen. The flowers are also bright yellow, pea-shaped, and make a cheerful display in mid-summer. They are the favourite haunt of large, colourful carpenter bees. By late summer the tree is draped with papery pods.
Propagation: Seed.
Uses: *Calpurnia* flowers at two years. Some specimens flower on and off for up to eight months. It also makes a passable miniature shade tree if space is at a premium, because its lowest branches appear fairly high up the trunk. Growth rate is at least 1 m per year for the first three years, the trunk thickening out afterwards. The tree's lifespan is short: get a replacement ready after five years. *Calpurnia* thrives in almost any summer climate, whether it is cool or warm, provided that rainfall is not too sparse.

Canthium mundianum
Rock alder, Klipels

Size: 4–7 x 3–6 m (wild), up to 5 x 5 m (garden)
Natural habitat: *Canthium* occurs over much of the east and south of the country. It is found in all sorts of deciduous woodland and in otherwise treeless grassland, but always among rocks and on slopes or cliff edges.
Growth form: It is an upright tree of unusual shape. The trunk is straight and slim; the branches are also straight and always protrude from the trunk slightly above the horizontal, and in opposite pairs. These pairs will in turn be at right angles to the next pair of branches, giving the young tree a striking, 'computer-built' appearance. The bark is smooth and almost white. In winter, when the tree is totally leafless, a community of these stark white sentinels among bare rocks is a very impressive sight. The flowers are white and small, but grow in large masses. The fruits have a characteristic lop-sided 'bokdrol' (goat dropping) appearance and are produced abundantly, attracting birds.
Propagation: Seed.
Uses: In cultivation *Canthium* grows about 60 cm per year. It makes a nice specimen, especially when planted in a large, steep rockery, and is ideal in a bird garden. It prefers low to moderate rainfall and looks its best when the winter is dry.

Attract birds Not only do bird baths make attractive features, but the birds enjoy them too. Regular cleaning keeps mosquitoes away. Shallow water is essential, as most garden birds have short legs and won't wade into deep water.

Cassia abbreviata
Long-tail cassia, Sjambok pod

Size: 3–7 x 2–6 m (wild), up to 5 x 5 m (garden)
Natural habitat: This species is found naturally in the eastern Lowveld. It occurs scattered in deciduous woodland.
Growth form: It is a smallish tree, with a rounded crown. The trunk is straight, and the bark deeply and regularly fissured. The flowers are glorious, large and pea-shaped, turning the whole tree yellow. They appear in early spring when the tree is leafless. The fruits are remarkable: thin cylindrical pods nearly a metre long that develop a spiral twist. These split, exposing the seeds, which are sought by barbets. Once all the seeds have fallen, the bright yellow interior of the pod is revealed. Empty pods hang on the tree in various stages of tatter for several months. This tree is host to the butterfly *Catopsilia florella*. 
Propagation: Seed. Young plants must be planted out quickly.
Uses: Flowering begins around five years. This tree thrives in many climates. It likes a warm summer with moderate to low rainfall, but copes with high rainfall, given good drainage, and flowers and fruits in a temperate climate. It is ideal for all but the tiniest gardens. Growth rate is about 60 cm per year.

Cassia petersiana
Monkey pod

Size: 2–4 x 2–3 m (wild), up to 3 x 3 m (garden)
Natural habitat: *C. petersiana* occurs naturally in Zululand and the eastern Lowveld. It is found in deciduous woodland, often alongside watercourses, and it frequently colonises road verges.
Growth form: It is sometimes shrubby, but may be a neat small tree. On older specimens the bark develops a snaking, branched fissure pattern, revealing the reddish underbark. The leaves are compound and droop gracefully. The flowers are pea-shaped, turning the whole tree yellow. The flowering period is long, extending from mid-summer to mid-winter. The fruits are long flat pods which, when still green and soft, are a source of food for birds. Grey louries, for example, break off long pieces that are swallowed whole, snake-fashion.
Propagation: Seed. Young plants do not grow well in pots and must be planted out quickly.
Uses: *C. petersiana* makes a nice small specimen given a warm summer with moderate rainfall. Growth rate in cultivation is rapid, about 80 cm per year initially, and flowering takes place in the second year.

Planting for a flower garden For red flowers, plant *Erythrina*, *Halleria* and *Schotia* in your garden; for blue, *Bolusanthus*; for white, *Rothmannia* or *Tabernaemontana*; for yellow, *Cassia* or *Peltophorum*.

Cassine aethiopica
Kooboo berry

Size: 3–8 x 3–8 m (wild), up to 4 x 4 m (garden)
Natural habitat: *C. aethiopica* is found naturally in much of the eastern half of South Africa. It occurs in a variety of wooded habitats but is most common in deciduous woodland.
Growth form: It is sometimes shrubby and, when single-stemmed, usually branches low down. The leaves are thickly textured and cast a dense shade. The flowers are small and white, but, when massed, make a pleasant display. The fruits are quite attractive and are produced in great numbers. They are about 2 cm in diameter, bright red, spherical and firmly fleshy. Larger fruit-eating birds, such as louries and parrots, enjoy them. They are reputed to be edible, but are rather bitter and astringent; definitely emergency rations only.
Propagation: Seed.
Uses: In cultivation *C. aethiopica* can be used as a screen or a filler in a bush clump, as well as a pleasing fruiting specimen. Cultivated specimens tend to be shrubby, at least for the first few years, unless pruned. Growth rate is about 50 cm per year. Fruiting begins at about six years, and occurs outside the natural range. Best results are obtained if the summer is warm and the rainfall moderate.

Cassine transvaalensis
Saffronwood, Ingwavuma

Size: 3–9 x 3–12 m (wild), up to 4 x 4 m (garden)
Natural habitat: This species occurs in the warmer, drier parts of the east. It is usually found in deciduous woodland. Some fine specimens can be seen in the Hluhluwe-Umfolozi Park, on the road between the main gate and Masinda.
Growth form: Typically, it is upright in form, although old trees develop a wide canopy. The leaves are thickly textured and cast a dense shade. The flowers are white and small, but make a pleasant display when massed. The attractive, yellow fruits are produced in abundance. They are about 2 cm in diameter, spherical and firmly fleshy. Larger fruit-eating birds such as louries and parrots enjoy them.
Propagation: Seed.
Uses: *C. transvaalensis* grows well in cultivation. Cultivated specimens tend to be shrubby, at least for the first few years, unless pruned. First fruiting occurs at about five years, and with a little attention *C. transvaalensis* makes a pleasant shade tree. It also makes a tub plant of character. Growth rate is modest, up to 50 cm per year. It enjoys a warm or temperate summer and moderate rainfall.

Watering after planting If it is ever necessary to water a tree after planting (see Introduction), NEVER give it a bucket of water or a quick splash with a hose. Adjust the hose to a tiny trickle, and leave it beside the tree for an hour or more. This way the water sinks in properly.

Celtis africana
Camdeboo stinkwood, White stinkwood

Size: 10–30 x 9–25 m (wild), up to 15 x 15 m (garden)
Natural habitat: This species is found over much of South Africa except the arid regions. It is common in mist-belt and coastal forests, and among rocks.
Growth form: It is a large, well-shaped tree with smooth, very pale bark. *C. africana* clearly reflects changing seasons. In spring, the new leaves are the palest green; mature foliage is darker and casts a good shade throughout summer; autumn leaves are yellow, particularly in a drier, cooler climate; and in winter *C. africana* almost gleams in the low-angled sunshine, its branches a tracery of white against a bright blue sky. Small dull orange berries are produced in large quantities during summer and are relished by birds. *C. africana* is also a haven for insects and is host to the butterfly *Libythea labdaca*.
Propagation: Seed – often dispersed by visiting birds.
Uses: *C. africana* combines year-round beauty, rapid growth, the ability to attract birds, and strong survival qualities. Growth rate is about 1 m per year, doubling in warm, wet summers. A respectable shade tree results at three years, and first fruit appears at four years. It withstands moderate drought and frost, making it particularly suitable for avenues and other exposed positions where a large tree is required quickly.

Celtis mildbraedii
Natal white stinkwood

Size: 10–22 x 10–25 m (wild), up to 14 x 15 m (garden)
Natural habitat: This is one of South Africa's rarest trees in the wild, being confined to a few isolated forest patches in KwaZulu-Natal. The best place to see *C. mildbraedii* is in Pigeon Valley in Durban.
Growth form: This is a very beautifully shaped tree with smooth, brown bark. The branches are characteristically held horizontally, and the lower trunk is embellished with spreading buttresses. *C. mildbraedii* has dark, glossy foliage. The fruits are large, shiny, orange berries which are a favourite food of the thickbilled weaver, and are sweet and tasty to the human palate too.
Propagation: Seed.
Uses: Although rare in the wild, this tree is readily available. Given warm, wet summers and frost-free winters, it performs as well in cultivation as it does in the wild. Growth rate is then about 1 m per year. An elegant shade tree results after six years, at which time the buttresses begin to develop and first fruiting occurs. Under marginal conditions, growth is much slower, and frost tolerance is probably nil.

Escaping fire Many of the trees living in shady forests do so simply to escape from fire. These 'fire refugees' grow very well when planted in the sun in a garden, where they are protected from fires.

Chaetacme aristata
Thorny elm

Size: 8–15 x 9–16 m (wild), up to 8 x 8 m (garden)
Natural habitat: *Chaetacme* ranges from Port Elizabeth northwards along the coastal plain, extending inland to the warmer, wetter parts of the east and north of the country. It occurs in coastal lowland forest and thickets.
Growth form: *Chaetacme* is a heavily built tree with a dense canopy. The main trunk is often fluted, or multi-stemmed, with fused trunks. All woody parts, including large trunks, bear fierce spines. Terminal branches have a regular and beautiful zig-zag pattern; the leaves are leathery and glossy, and most attractive. The fruits may cover the tree and make a lovely display. They are fleshy and about 1.5 cm in diameter, pale pinkish-orange, with a translucent quality. Louries and fruit bats eat them. *Chaetacme* is an important butterfly plant, and is host to *Charaxes cithaeron* and *C. xiphares*.
Propagation: Seed.
Uses: *Chaetacme* casts a particularly deep shade, ideal where a cooling effect is required, but a bit overwhelming otherwise. It makes a good tall screen in a large garden. Growth is fairly fast, about 70 cm per year. First fruiting can be expected at seven years. *Chaetacme* grows best where rainfall is moderate to high and the summer is warm.

Chrysophyllum viridifolium
Fluted milkwood

Size: 10–25 x 10–20 m (wild), up to 17 x 16 m (garden)
Natural habitat: *Chrysophyllum* occurs naturally on the KwaZulu-Natal coast. It is found in coastal lowland forest and is common locally, for example, in Pigeon Valley in Durban.
Growth form: It is a magnificent tall, evergreen tree with a long straight trunk and spreading canopy. The trunk is heavily fluted in the fashion of a stalactite or a cluster of organ-pipes. The leaves are dark and neatly veined. The fruits resemble miniature pumpkins. At first green, they turn yellow and finally brown before falling. Monkeys and fruit bats eat the soft parts, discarding the large polished, chestnut-coloured seeds that form a spangled mosaic on the forest floor. *Chrysophyllum* is host to the butterflies *Pseudacraea eurytus* and *P. lucretia*, and the rare *Euryphura achlys*.
Propagation: Seed, but results are irregular. Otherwise, harvest tiny seedlings from beneath a mature tree.
Uses: A nice shade tree results after about seven years, and trunk fluting begins then. Fruiting begins at about 10 years within the natural range; outside the range, and in a dry climate, a first and prolific fruiting was noted at 18 years. Given a warm summer with high rainfall, growth is fairly rapid, about 70 cm per year.

Wild seedlings You can often find wild-grown seedlings near the parent tree (only harvest them with the land-owner's permission, though). After rain, lift seedlings out by hand. If the root comes out intact, the seedling will survive. The smallest seedlings are the ones most likely to transplant successfully.

Cladostemon kirkii
Three-finger bush

Size: 3–7 x 4–8 m (wild), up to 4 x 4 m (garden)
Natural habitat: *Cladostemon* is highly localised in South Africa, being confined to woodlands and dry forests in the Lebombo Mountains and surrounds in northern Zululand.
Growth form: It is a small tree with a wide canopy spread. The foliage droops gracefully. *Cladostemon* bears exquisite flowers in spring. They are large, and initially white. Soon they change colour, as the yesterday-today-and-tomorrow does, turning deep yellow. This phase is relatively long lasting, so a flowering tree is mostly yellow. The upper two petals are larger that the lower two, creating the look of a butterfly. The fruits resemble small knobkerries with a matte finish. Ripe fruits develop a penetrating smell once picked, and are not a good addition to an ornamental dried fruit arrangement!
Propagation: Seed or root cuttings.
Uses: *Cladostemon* is one of the finest of all the small ornamental trees. Within its natural range a 10-year-old tree reached 4 m in height, and first flowered and fruited at four years. Fruiting has been observed outside the natural range, but only after nine years. *Cladostemon* will only thrive where the summer is warm and the climate fairly dry.

Clerodendrum glabrum
Verbena tree, White cat's whiskers

Size: 3–9 x 3–7 m (wild), up to 6 x 5 m (garden)
Natural habitat: This tree, found almost everywhere in the eastern half of the country, is equally happy in tall evergreen forest, deciduous woodland, and on koppies or coastal dunes.
Growth form: It is a smallish tree, occasionally erect and shapely, more usually lanky or shrubby. On older specimens the bark develops a beautiful cracked, striated pattern. The flowers are small, but are borne in dense cauliflower-like masses. They may be white or lilac. Their scent is pleasant when fresh, getting much sharper with age. These flowers are perhaps the best of all for attracting insects. Brightly coloured beetles like them. So do butterflies, such as *Hypolycaena philippus*, which also breeds on *Clerodendrum*. The flowers are followed by shiny black berries, beloved by small birds.
Propagation: Seed.
Uses: *Clerodendrum* is not a conventional garden beauty, but its ability to attract insects and birds makes it ideal in a bird garden. Flowering begins at three years. On a large scale it can be used to rehabilitate eroded watercourses. It is especially useful because of its tolerance of a wide climatic range. *Clerodendrum* grows about 1.5 m per year if the summer is wet and warm.

Storing seed When collecting seed from fruit, separate it from the rest of the fruit, whether it is to be stored or planted. Soft fruit rapidly becomes mouldy and the fungus can kill the seeds. Also, the moisture in the fruit can sometimes trigger germination before the seed is in a suitable position for growth.

Cola greenwayi
Hairy cola

Size: 3–6 x 2–5 m (wild), up to 4 x 3 m (garden)
Natural habitat: *Cola* has a very restricted distribution in Zululand. This tree is most common in sand forest, occurring sparingly in other evergreen forests. *Cola* lives much of its life in partial shade.
Growth form: It is upright in form, and the branches usually sweep vertically upwards, giving the tree a column-like appearance. The bark of a mature *Cola* tree is wonderfully marbled in brown, green and grey. The tree has pleasing foliage. New growth forms thin pyramids, the pale golden-green leaves hanging vertically. The tree's fruits are orange and furry, and most attractive.
Propagation: Seed.
Uses: *Cola* makes a nice specimen, which does not take up too much space. This tree has not yet fruited outside its natural range. Initial growth is slow, but speeds up after a year or so, producing a 2-m specimen after six years. It grows best in full sun and retains its unique growth form there. The tree does well in a warm summer with moderate to good rainfall, but withstands moderate drought. An exotic relative is the source of the cola that was part of the original *Coca-Cola®* recipe.

Colophospermum mopane
Mopane

Size: 4–11 x 3–8 m (wild), up to 6 x 5 m (garden)
Natural habitat: The mopane is found naturally in the far northeast, where it occurs in low-altitude deciduous woodland. It is frequently dominant and may cover the landscape.
Growth form: The mopane is usually a well-formed tree. The shrubby form seen in parts of the Lowveld is the result of local soil conditions. The bark is handsome, dark, and ruggedly fissured. The leaves are also attractive, shaped like a deeply cloven hoof. Sweeping veins, arranged like a magnetic field, emphasise the shape. The leaves are the food of the caterpillar *Gonimbrasia belina*, the 'mopane worm', a fearsome, spiny creature decked out in black, blue and yellow. Its autumn feasts are accompanied by an enthusiastic munching sound. Leaves that escape turn a rich russet over winter before being shed. The fruit is a small kidney-shaped pod containing a single seed resembling a flattened brain.
Propagation: Seed, to be planted while still inside its pod.
Uses: The mopane makes a pleasant specimen and foliage tree. Growth rate may be slow initially, accelerating later, even up to 1 m per year. It tolerates fairly high rainfall, but looks best if rainfall is poor to moderate, as the lovely winter colours develop only if there is a long dry period.

Germinating Plant seeds to a depth equal to their own length, in a loose, crumbly seedling mix. Good drainage is essential. Keep the soil moist, not wet, and shade from harsh sun. Don't give up too easily – some species take up to a year to germinate.

Combretum erythrophyllum
River bushwillow

Size: 6–17 x 6–15 m (wild), up to 12 x 10 m (garden)
Natural habitat: This tree is widespread in the eastern half of South Africa, usually occurring along riverbanks.
Growth form: It is a spreading tree, which often leans at impossible angles, as a result of being battered by floods. Branches often fork into threes, creating firm foundations for thrush's nest sites. Canaries strip soft fibres from twigs to use as nest lining. New spring growth is a delicate pale green, sometimes interspersed with white. Autumn begins in April with a few yellow leaves, and persists into July, when the remaining leaves are red. Fruits appear in pink masses in late autumn. They have the texture of fine cardboard, and form miniature, four-winged mobiles, designed to assist wind-dispersal. The seeds are often parasitised. The southern black tit finds the parasites by tapping the fruit to detect hollow spaces, holding the fruit firmly in its feet in order to rip it open.
Propagation: Seed, which must be unparasitised.
Uses: *C. erythrophyllum* is valuable in cold areas. It makes an ideal shade tree, or an unconventional bird tree. It can be used in avenues, as has been done in Kimberley, or alongside dams and streams. Growth rate is 1 m or more per year. Mature fruits can be used in dried flower arrangements.

Combretum imberbe
Leadwood, Hardekool

Size: 10–20 x 8–20 m (wild), up to 11 x 10 m (garden)
Natural habitat: *C. imberbe* is found naturally in the Lowveld. It occurs in dry woodland, usually near small watercourses.
Growth form: It is a large, striking tree with a long, clean main trunk topped by a dense mass of heavy branches. The bark is a distinctive pale grey with close, regular, vertical furrows. The fruits are small and pale yellow. They have the typical *Combretum* texture and appearance of fine cardboard, and are shaped like miniature, four-winged mobiles. This popular Lowveld tree is as famous dead as alive. Dead specimens last for years, and stand dotted all over the veld in suitable habitats. Their knot-holes and hollow branches provide nest sites for many birds and other animals.
Propagation: Seed, which must be unparasitised.
Uses: This tree, with its mighty bearing and beautiful bark, is widely admired. Unfortunately, it is a slow performer in cultivation. Under ideal conditions where there is a hot summer, moderate rainfall and a frost-free winter, the growth rate is 50 cm per year. Under poorer conditions growth is much slower. Nevertheless, *C. imberbe* is worth growing as a specimen, if only for posterity. Mature fruits can be used in dried flower arrangements.

Spring colours The phenomenon of new spring leaves being red, brown, purple, blue or white results from different rates of production of the various leaf pigments. When chlorophyll (the green pigment) is produced last, the other colours get a turn first, and can be seen in the tree's leaves. A number of indigenous trees display these colour flushes.

Combretum kraussii
Forest bushwillow

Size: 8–25 x 7–20 m (wild), up to 9 x 9 m (garden)
Natural habitat: This tree occurs over much of the eastern part of the country. It is found in evergreen forest and in thick, bushy habitats where rainfall is high.
Growth form: It is upright, with a dense canopy. *C. kraussii* is leafless for only about a month. Its seasonal colour changes are remarkable. New spring leaves are white, advertising flowers that appear simultaneously. As spring advances the foliage turns pale green. Mature leaves are dark green, interspersed with the occasional bright red leaf. The proportion of red leaves increases as autumn approaches, until all are shed. Fruiting sees a fiery pink blush diffusing throughout the canopy in late summer. Fruits have the typical *Combretum* texture of fine cardboard, and form small, four-winged mobiles. As with *C. erythrophyllum*, seed parasites attract southern black tits.
Propagation: Seed, which must be unparasitised.
Uses: *C. kraussii* can be used as a specimen, to provide shade, as background foliage, or to create a tall, dense screen. Growth is fairly fast, about 80 cm per year in a warm area. *C. kraussii* likes moderate to good rainfall but survives an average winter drought. Mature fruits can be used in dried flower arrangements.

Combretum molle
Velvet bushwillow

Size: 3–8 x 3–9 m (wild), up to 5 x 5 m (garden)
Natural habitat: *C. molle* occurs over much of the eastern third of South Africa in dry woodland, often among rocks. 
Growth form: It is single-stemmed, though usually small and craggy. The leaves have a distinctive velvet texture. In colder areas autumn leaves turn purple, but in the warm Lowveld various shades of rusty orange are seen. The flowers are sweetly scented and grow profusely in early spring when the tree is leafless. Nectar-seeking insects enjoy them and *C. molle* is host to the butterfly *Hamanumida daedalus*. Fruits have the texture of fine cardboard, and form miniature, four-winged mobiles. At first pale green, they turn red, and mature to yellow-brown with a satin sheen. Lesser masked weavers and southern black tits inspect them for parasites. Canaries pull fibrous bark strips from young twigs for their nests.
Propagation: Seed, which must be unparasitised.
Uses: *C. molle* makes a nice specimen, and a position in a warm north-facing rockery is ideal. Rate of growth is about 40 cm per year. *C. molle* does best with moderate rainfall. Mature fruits can be used in dried flower arrangements.

Choosing your tree When choosing a tree at the nursery, go for a well-formed specimen with blemish-free leaves, a thick stem, and a strong growing point (this is the leading shoot that grows upwards). The tallest tree is not necessarily the best.

Combretum zeyheri
Large-fruited bushwillow, Raasblaar

Size: 3–5 x 3–5 m (wild), up to 4 x 4 m (garden)
Natural habitat: This species is found in the warmer parts of the east. It occurs in deciduous woodland, often on rocky hills.
Growth form: It is a small tree, sometimes with two or three stems. Its leaves make a rasping sound in the wind, hence its Afrikaans name. The fruits are typical of *Combretum*, having the texture of fine cardboard, and form miniature, four-winged mobiles. *C. zeyheri* has the largest fruits of any local *Combretum*. Southern black tits explore the fruits, looking for parasites. The fruits mature to a rich brown in early winter and contrast beautifully with the deep yellow of the ageing leaves. The gold splashes in the muted yellow autumn landscape found in the southern Kruger National Park are due to *C. zeyheri*. 
Propagation: Seed, which must be unparasitised.
Uses: This tree makes a nice foliage and fruiting specimen. It needs warm summers with moderate rainfall and dry, virtually frost-free winters. Fruiting and autumn foliage displays only develop well in these conditions. Growth rate is about 40 cm per year. Mature fruits look good in dried flower arrangements.

Commiphora harveyi
Bronze paper commiphora

Size: 3–10 x 2–8 m (wild), up to 8 x 7 m (garden)
Natural habitat: This species is confined to the warmer parts of the east. It is usually found on hot, north-facing slopes, often among rocks, and can be common in coastal forest.
Growth form: *C. harveyi* is upright with a fairly straight trunk. It is one of the most attractive of all indigenous trees, having a gleaming copper-coloured bark that peels in wafer-thin layers to reveal the bronze-green underbark. The tree's foliage is graceful, and autumn sees an extended display of bright, yet pale, yellow. Fruits are spherical and about 1 cm in diameter, ripening to red. They attract birds, which split the outer casing in half and let the two halves fall away. The shiny black seed remains behind, held by a bright red, claw-like aril, that looks just like a small red hand holding out a tidbit to the bird. Only female trees bear fruit. Fruiting is a bit irregular, but in a good year all manner of birds are attracted to the rich food supply.
Propagation: Seed or cuttings.
Uses: *C. harveyi* has decorative value and makes a good shade tree. Growth rate is about 1 m per year if the summer is warm. It enjoys dry heat, although it can tolerate a little frost and does thrive in damp areas. *C. harveyi* grows well in pots and makes an excellent bonsai.

Pot plants People without gardens can still enjoy indigenous trees, as they make wonderful pot plants, and many species flower well when potted. The larger the pot, the larger the tree will grow. *Acacia*, *Commiphora*, *Cussonia*, and *Ficus* all do well in pots.

Commiphora neglecta
Sweet-root commiphora

Size: 3–5 x 3–5 m (wild), up to 4 x 4 m (garden)
Natural habitat: *C. neglecta* is locally common in Zululand, in flat, low-lying areas where the soil is sandy, and in the warmer parts of the northeast.
Growth form: This tree is small and craggy. The main trunk is short, and branching is angular and stiff. Each branch ends in a sharp spine. The delicate leaves are a rich shiny green. The bark is dazzling, varying from turquoise to lime green, even on one tree, depending upon how recently it has peeled. Fruits are spherical and about 1 cm in diameter. They ripen to red. This attracts birds, which split the outer casing in half, the two halves falling away. The shiny black seed remains behind, held by a bright red, claw-like aril. Only female trees bear fruit.
Propagation: Seed or cuttings.
Uses: *C. neglecta* makes a beautiful specimen, provided that it is given a hot, dry spot out of reach of frost. It grows well in pots and makes an excellent bonsai. The tree grows 50 cm or more per year, fruiting when three years old. If the tree is planted in a flowerbed, damage to the roots is inevitable as neighbouring weeds are removed, and this induces suckering. New trees sprout from the damaged roots, and a wild community is reproduced.

Commiphora pyracanthoides
Kanniedood

Size: 3–4 x 3–4 m (wild), up to 3 x 3 m (garden)
Natural habitat: This species is fairly widespread in the hotter parts of the north and east, and occurs on rocky hillsides as well as in sandy lowlands, where it may form thickets.
Growth form: Young trees branch in an angular fashion, but as they mature a relatively clean trunk develops, topped with a slightly spreading crown. All branches are tipped with strong spines. The leaves are at their best in spring, when the new growth is red. The long leafless period enhances the effect of the tree's shape and bark. The bark peels in shiny layers, varying in colour from yellow to grey. The fruits are typical of *Commiphora*. They are spherical and about 1 cm in diameter, and ripen to red. The colour attracts birds, which split the outer casing in half and let the two halves fall away. The shiny black seed remains behind, held by a bright red, claw-like aril. Only female trees bear fruit.
Propagation: Seed or cuttings.
Uses: It is ideal for a rockery where it would make a nice contrast with species typical of its natural habitat, such as aloes and other succulents. Given hot, dry conditions *C. pyracanthoides* grows about 50 cm a year. It grows well in pots and makes an excellent bonsai.

***Commiphora* in history** The genus *Commiphora* has its roots in history. The myrrh of the Bible is a resin derived from an Arabian species. The resin of other species provided incense, and Queen Hatsheput, who reigned in Egypt in about 1500 BC, imported incense trees from Somalia.

Commiphora schimperi
Glossy-leaved commiphora

Size: 3–5 x 2–4 m (wild), up to 4 x 3 m (garden)
Natural habitat: This species occurs widely in the warm parts of the northeast. In KwaZulu-Natal it is common on the hot, rocky hills south of Pongola.
Growth form: It has a highly characteristic growth habit. The trunk is straight and slender by *Commiphora* standards, and the branches weave stiffly in all directions in the style of Medusa's locks. *C. schimperi* has neatly toothed leaflets and the bark varies from lime green to yellow-green, sometimes with a yellow-grey outer crust. The fruits have the same fascinating design as is typical of *Commiphora*. They are spherical and about 1 cm in diameter. They ripen to red. The colour attracts birds, which split the outer casing in half and let the two halves fall away. The shiny black seed remains behind, held by a bright red, claw-like aril. Only female trees bear fruit.
Propagation: Seed or cuttings.
Uses: This tree makes an exceptionally attractive specimen. It needs hot, dry conditions, a baking north-facing slope being ideal. Large specimens transplant well, as with all other *Commiphora* species, a boon for instant landscaping. It also grows well in pots and makes an excellent bonsai.

Cordia caffra
Septee

Size: 4–9 x 3–6 m (wild), up to 7 x 5 m (garden)
Natural habitat: *Cordia* is found naturally in the warmer parts of the east. It occurs in all sorts of evergreen forest, including swamp and dune forests.
Growth form: It is usually an upright tree with a fairly narrow canopy and may be briefly deciduous. The leaves are poplar-like, hanging from long stalks and fluttering in the slightest breeze. The bark is striking and unusual. It is a variety of shades of very pale brown, having a 'peeled' appearance reminiscent of a guava trunk. *Cordia*'s flowers are small white bells, attractive but short-lived. It produces an abundant crop of bright orange, fleshy, sticky fruits in summer; birds eat these.
Propagation: Seed.
Uses: *Cordia* is worth growing for its bark, foliage and fruits. A nice specimen can be expected at five years. First flowering occurs sometimes as early as three years, fruiting at about five years. Growth is rapid, about 1 m per year in a warm climate. *C. caffra* enjoys high rainfall but withstands some drought. It is frost-sensitive.

Bird homes By virtue of their size, strength and powers of endurance, trees provide shelter. They are the most important of all nest and roost sites for birds. The shade cast is welcomed by people and animals alike, sheltering them from the hottest sun and reducing the effect of cold winds.

Craibia zimmermannii
Craibia

Size: 3–8 x 3–9 m (wild), up to 5 x 5 m (garden)
Natural habitat: *Craibia* is found naturally in Zululand where it occurs in sandy soils, typically as a constituent of sand forest.
Growth form: It is usually a small, neatly shaped, evergreen tree. This tree is very upright when young, but develops a spreading canopy when mature, if given space. The leaves are asymmetrically compound and elegant. The flowers are outstanding, white and pea-shaped, quite large and strongly scented. The fruit is a hard, woody pod that explodes when mature, scattering the seed.
Propagation: Seed, which must be collected before the pods split and scatter it. Seed can be stored for long periods, but then needs to be soaked in hot water or abraded.
Uses: *Craibia* makes a wonderful and reliable small foliage and flowering specimen, and miniature shade tree. Growth rate is moderate, about 50 cm per year, but first flowering sometimes occurs at two years. It is equally at home in low or high rainfall areas. Despite being confined to sand in the wild, it grows well in most soils.

Croton gratissimus
Lavender croton, Bergboegoe

Size: 3–15 x 3–15 m (wild), up to 7 x 8 m – in really exceptional cases, up to 14 m (garden)
Natural habitat: This species is fairly widespread in the warmer parts of the north and east of the country, and occurs in woodland and sand forest.
Growth form: *C. gratissimus* is a small, elegant tree, which eventually develops a spreading canopy. The leaves are typical *Croton*, silvery-white beneath, with scattered rusty spots creating a pepper-and-salt effect, contrasting with the glossy green of the upper-surface. The tree is evergreen, but continuously sheds leaves a few at a time. Ageing leaves turn a beautiful orange and remain on the tree for several weeks, so that the green and silver is always flecked with orange. The flowers are small, white pompons and have a modest charm. The fruits are attractive three-lobed capsules.
Propagation: Seed.
Uses: *C. gratissimus* can be used as part of a mixed screen, but it is well worth pride of place as both a form and foliage specimen. This tree grows fairly quickly, about 70 cm per year. *C. gratissimus* likes high rainfall and sandy soil, but nevertheless tolerates all soils and is very drought-hardy.

Preparing seeds 'Fire treatment' is easily provided for seeds requiring great heat to induce germination. Pile dry grass over a heap of seeds and set fire to it. There are bound to be seeds that get the right amount of scorch – whether on the outside or inside of the heap.

Croton sylvaticus
Forest croton

Size: 10–25 x 10–25 m (wild), up to 16 x 18 m (garden)
Natural habitat: *C. sylvaticus* is fairly widespread in the warmer parts of the north and east of the country. It is common in the lowland forests of coastal KwaZulu-Natal.
Growth form: This is usually a large spreading tree, but towards the north of its range it tends to be smaller and shrubby. Unlike most other species of *Croton*, its leaves are green on both their upper and under surfaces, and it is more or less deciduous. However, the fruits are bright orange and produced in profusion, creating a fine display in late summer. Many insects enjoy *C. sylvaticus* and it is host to the butterfly *Charaxes candiope*.
Propagation: Seed.
Uses: This is a very useful species in cultivation. It makes a fine shade tree and its deciduous character is an advantage in cooler areas where winter sun is needed. In warm winters the tree is rarely completely leafless. It grows very rapidly, 1.2 m or more per year. Best performance can be expected where rainfall is high. Although confined to frost-free areas in the wild, *C. sylvaticus* can tolerate mild frost.

Cryptocarya woodii
Cape laurel

Size: 8–25 x 8–20 m (wild), up to 8 x 7 m (garden)
Natural habitat: *Cryptocarya* extends from the Eastern Cape through KwaZulu-Natal to the eastern Escarpment. This tree is common, sometimes dominant, in mist-belt forest.
Growth form: It can be a tall tree, reaching the forest canopy, but more often is short and chunky, on the forest margin. The leaves are dark and glossy, and are rounded, with greatly elongated tips. They exude a rich smell of myrtle when crushed. The tree's fruits, which are eaten by birds, are spherical, black and glossy, and make a fine display. *Cryptocarya* is host to two species of butterfly, *Charaxes xiphares* and *Papilio euphranor*.
Propagation: Seed, which must be fresh.
Uses: *Cryptocarya* is a fine garden subject, the shape and smell of the leaves always providing a talking point. The growth rate is moderate, about 50 cm per year, but a pretty specimen results after five years. First fruiting can be expected then. *Cryptocarya* grows best where rainfall is high, but copes with moderate rainfall, provided the summer is fairly cool.

Insect life All bird foods, be they fruit, seeds, nectar or insects, are provided directly or indirectly by plants. Trees indigenous to your particular area have, over the ages, evolved along with the insects living there and so support more insects than alien trees, which have not had time to adjust to local conditions.

Cunonia capensis
Rooiels

Size: 6–18 x 5–16 m (wild), up to 10 x 9 m (garden)
Natural habitat: *Cunonia* ranges from the southwest Cape to KwaZulu-Natal, always in areas of high rainfall. This tree is confined to evergreen forests and is most abundant alongside streams.
Growth form: *Cunonia* is erect in form, and, when a mature tree, bears a good canopy. This species is evergreen and has attractive, compound leaves, with dark, glossy, neatly serrated leaflets. The growing points are enclosed by semi-circular red stipules. *Cunonia* has beautiful white flowers that are produced in long, erect, catkin-like spikes.
Propagation: Seed. This is very fine and must be sown directly onto the growing medium and not covered.
Uses: *Cunonia* makes a nice specimen, even when small, because it constantly produces its unusual stipules. Flowering begins at about four years. The ideal is to plant it next to a natural water feature. Growth is reasonably fast, about 60 cm per year, provided that rainfall is good and the summer cool or temperate. This tree can withstand some frost, but will languish in heat or drought.

Curtisia dentata
Assegai tree

Size: 7–10 x 6–8 m (wild), up to 8 x 6 m (garden)
Natural habitat: *Curtisia* is found naturally in the wetter parts of the country, ranging from the southwest Cape to the eastern Escarpment. This tree occurs almost exclusively in temperate evergreen forest, near the coast in the Cape, and in the mist-belt further north.
Growth form: It is a slender, upright tree that rarely spreads very much. The foliage is handsome. The leaves are glossy bluish-green above, velvety yellow-green with ginger veins below, and neatly toothed in the fashion of the English beech. The flowers are insignificant but the fruits are distinctive, white berries relished by birds.
Propagation: Seed, but results are erratic.
Uses: *Curtisia* makes an elegant form and foliage specimen. Even in later life, this tree does not outgrow a small garden because its canopy stays within bounds. If close-planted, it can be used as a tall screen, because many lower branches are retained. Fruit appears only in cooler gardens. Growth is reasonably fast, about 60 cm per year. *Curtisia* enjoys high rainfall and a temperate summer, and dislikes heat. The tree can tolerate moderate frost. It grows well in a tub and, as the foliage lasts well when cut, makes an adequate Christmas tree.

Flower colour The majority of South African trees have white flowers, some showy and some small and insignificant. The white colour of the petals is due to the absence of pigment. The intensity of whiteness is caused by air spaces within the petal tissue, which reflect light.

Cussonia natalensis
Simple-leaved cabbage tree

Size: 3–8 x 3–10 m (wild), up to 6 x 7 m (garden)
Natural habitat: *C. natalensis* is scattered throughout the eastern half of KwaZulu-Natal and from there northwards, wherever there are hot, rocky slopes. 
Growth form: This is the finest of all cabbage trees. Unlike its relatives, it develops a spreading canopy. The bark is thick and fissured. *C. natalensis* has beautiful, maple-like leaves. As winter approaches they turn brilliant, yet pale, yellow before falling. The fruits are dull red to black in colour and produced on long spikes, which protrude from the canopy, rather like the arms of a candelabra. They are highly sought-after by birds.
Propagation: Seed, which must be fresh. It grows best if planted out when small, but also grows well in a pot.
Uses: *C. natalensis* makes an outstanding specimen. Older trees have dead branches or decaying knot-holes easily excavated by barbets and woodpeckers, so are important nest sites. Growth rate is over 1 m per year. *C. natalensis* likes warm dry conditions, and does not produce autumn colours if the winter is too wet.

Cussonia paniculata
Mountain cabbage tree

Size: 2–7 x 1–5 m (wild), up to 4 x 3 m (garden)
Natural habitat: *C. paniculata* is found in the eastern interior, including the cold uplands. It occurs on rocky slopes, in open grassland and in small bush clumps.
Growth form: Young trees are unbranched, but the trunk may fork once or twice in later life. The bark is thick and fissured. The very attractive leaves are a rich bluish-green, and the leaf fingers are sharply serrated. The flowers are small, greenish, and borne in long spikes. The fruits, produced on the same spikes, are dull red to black, and are popular with birds. After flowering and fruiting, the tree tends to branch at the growing point or die back a bit and put out branches lower on the trunk.
Propagation: Seed, which must be fresh.
Uses: The unusual growth form adds a new texture to garden structure. Growth rate is 80 cm per year. Fruiting begins around eight years. *C. paniculata* likes warm summers, wet or dry, but must have dry winters. It is not as hardy as it might appear in the wild – over-watering in winter can kill it. Trees growing in apparently very frosty areas such as the high Drakensberg are usually found on steep, north-facing slopes or cradled by rocks. By contrast, a new bare garden may be far more hostile. The tree can be protected by planting tougher shelter plants first.

Life cycles A dead tree does not imply that the gardener is slacking in duty. A tree has fulfilled only half its ecological potential while alive. After death it functions as a slow-release system for vital nutrients, which are needed by all sorts of interesting invertebrates.

Cussonia spicata
Cabbage tree, Kiepersol

Size: 2–12 x 1–13 m (wild), up to 6 x 6 m (garden)
Natural habitat: This is the most widespread cabbage tree, being found almost everywhere in the east and south of the country. It is common in cool grassland, in the mountains and the Highveld, and in dry woodlands.
Growth form: Young trees are single-stemmed, but older specimens may have a massive trunk with a dense, branching crown. Branching commences when the tree is 2–4 m tall. It can be induced if the factors that produce it in the wild are simulated. Fire and browsing both contribute to branching by causing temporary damage to the growing points, and so many of the specimens with the most character often have dassies contentedly nibbling their new growth. The fruits are dull red to black, and produced on long spikes, rather like the arms of a candelabra. They are much sought-after by birds.
Propagation: Seed, which must be fresh.
Uses: The unusual growth form adds a new texture to garden structure. Growth rate is about 80 cm per year. Fruiting begins at about eight years. Dead branches and decaying knot-holes on older trees are excavated by barbets and woodpeckers, and are important nest sites. *C. spicata* prefers high rainfall. In mild winters it is evergreen. It is only slightly frost-hardy.

Cyathea dregei
Tree fern

Size: 2–9 x 1–3 m (wild), up to 8 x 3 m (garden)
Natural habitat: Tree ferns range from the southern Cape to the eastern Escarpment, wherever there is high rainfall or abundant groundwater. They invariably occur along drainage lines, sometimes in forest shade.
Growth form: Tree ferns are instantly recognisable by their mop of huge leaves atop a bare cylindrical trunk. They lack both flowers and fruits, the hallmarks of modern plants. They reproduce using spores, produced in brown patches on the back of the leaves. Malachite sunbirds often nest in tree ferns.
Propagation: Spores, which must be sprinkled onto porous material, such as moss, and kept permanently damp. To do this, cover with glass until germination takes place. Slight shade and a temperature of 17–20 °C give best results.
Uses: Tree ferns look perfect beside water but are difficult to keep in prime condition. They must have high rainfall or a very damp – but not waterlogged – substrate. Partial shade helps. Growth rate is 5–10 cm per year, depending upon climate. However, leaves grow large and luxuriant even on a small plant. Tree ferns tolerate some frost, but it blackens the leaves for several months. Note that large tree ferns dug from the veld nearly always die within two years.

Creative planting Make a statement in form – plant three different *Cussonia* species in one hole. Then wait to see which one will grow upwards, and which two outwards and sideways.

Dais cotinifolia
Pompon tree

Size: 3–10 x 2–8 m (wild), up to 7 x 6 m (garden)
Natural habitat: *Dais* is common and familiar within its fairly restricted range, which extends from the Eastern Cape to the eastern Escarpment. It is found in evergreen forests, alongside streams, and in thornveld, usually in the thicker patches of foliage among rocks.
Growth form: It is a slender tree, sometimes multi-stemmed. The leaves are quite attractive, pale green with a velvety feel. In areas with a cool, dry winter the leaves turn a cheerful yellow before being shed. *Dais* has pretty, pale pink pompon flowers, which appear in profusion in mid-summer.
Propagation: Seed.
Uses: *Dais* is well worth growing as a flowering specimen, although its beauty has been rather over-eulogised. The tree's flowering display retains its pristine freshness only until the first rain, which is likely within days of the opening of the flowers. Growth is rapid, up to 1 m per year. First flowering occurs at about three years. *Dais* can be trained into a small shade tree and has even been used, with fair effect, as an avenue tree. *Dais* dislikes drought.

Deinbollia oblongifolia
Dune soap-berry

Size: 2–9 x 1–6 m (wild), up to 7 x 4 m (garden)
Natural habitat: *Deinbollia* occurs naturally on the KwaZulu-Natal coast. Most typically it occurs in dune forest.
Growth form: It is a small, stiff tree, bearing a tight mop of large leaves. The small, almost spherical, flowers are white with a faint violet tinge. They are borne in tall pyramids, often packed so closely together that they resemble space-age cluster-housing. The fruits are large, yellow-orange berries, massed together, and loved by birds. *Deinbollia* is also one of the best butterfly trees. The caterpillars of the very beautiful *Euxanthe wakefieldi* and *Euphaedra neophron* depend upon its foliage. *Deudorix* caterpillars are remarkable for feeding upon the developing fruit. The adult caterpillars and other butterfly species feed on sap oozing from small bark wounds.
Propagation: Seed.
Uses: *Deinbollia* makes a pretty specimen, ideal for a small garden. Flowering and fruiting begin in the second year, even outside the natural range. The fruits persist on the tree, birds permitting, for several months in autumn, making *Deinbollia* excellent for a bird garden. Growth rate is about 30 cm per year. Although confined in the wild to a warm, wet climate and sandy soil, *Deinbollia* thrives in quite low rainfall and shale.

Avenue trees Trees with large or messy fruits, or spiny branches, do not make good avenue trees. Scale is important when choosing an avenue tree. Mixing species in an avenue is rarely successful, as it detracts from the impact. Don't alternate evergreen and deciduous trees; it looks spotty.

Dichrostachys cinerea
Sickle bush, Sekelbos

Size: 2–5 x 3–6 m (wild), up to 3 x 4 m (garden)
Natural habitat: *Dichrostachys* occurs naturally in the warmer parts of KwaZulu-Natal and the northeast. This tree is common in deciduous woodland and may form thickets where overgrazing prevents grass fires.
Growth form: It is a small, scrappy tree, sometimes relatively shrub-like, with a strong resemblance to the acacias. Some books describe it as thornless, an impression not shared by those falling into its clutches. It certainly lacks the thorns that distinguish acacias, but each branch tip ends in a sharp spine. The flowers are extremely pretty, fluffy and bi-coloured, half pink, half yellow, and they hang like fancy decorations. The fruits are pods, produced in convoluted bunches.
Propagation: Seed or cuttings.
Uses: *Dichrostachys* does not make a prize specimen, but is worth growing for its unique flowers that appear at four years. It is best placed on the sunny edge of a bush clump, where the flowers will look their best. Growth is reasonably fast, about 70 cm per year. *Dichrostachys* attracts small insects, and hence warblers and robins, so can be included in a wildlife garden. It likes a warm summer, wet or dry. It also makes a good bonsai.

Diospyros mespiliformis
Jackal-berry, Jakkalsbessie

Size: 8–25 x 7–25 m (wild), up to 10 x 10 m (garden)
Natural habitat: This is found in the Lowveld and is common alongside all the smaller watercourses in the Kruger Park.
Growth form: *D. mespiliformis* is tall and upright in growth form and evergreen, with a dense canopy. New leaves, particularly on young trees, are flaming red. The trunk is elegant and straight, with dark, fissured bark. The fruits are reputed to be purple when mature but louries, parrots and green pigeons seldom seem to allow them to progress beyond green. Beneath a fruiting tree the constant splat of falling skins, seeds and whole fruits attracts warthogs in the wild. Fruits are borne only on female trees.
Propagation: Seed.
Uses: *D. mespiliformis* makes a magnificent shade and specimen tree. It grows at a rate of about 60 cm per year, once established in an environment with a warm summer and moderate rainfall or a high water table. First fruiting can be expected at about seven years, but has yet to be noted outside the natural range. *D. mespiliformis* tolerates slight frost. The edible persimmon is a relative and so are several species that produce ebony.

Pruning large trees Don't try to turn a large tree into a small tree by constant pruning. It will always look contrived and tortured. Rather use a smaller tree in the first place.

Diospyros natalensis
Small-leaved jackal-berry

Size: 2–10 x 2–10 m (wild), up to 6 x 5 m (garden)
Natural habitat: *D. natalensis* occurs naturally on the coast and immediate hinterland of KwaZulu-Natal and the Eastern Cape. It is fairly common in dune forest, but rarer in other evergreen forests, where it is found mainly on the fringes.
Growth form: This can be an upright tree with weeping branches, but is often shrubby. *D. natalensis* has tiny, glossy, very neat leaves. The spring flush may be russet or gold, and the flowers are small white bells. The fruits appear in mid-winter and are exceptionally pretty. They are orange and are borne in cups, so resemble acorns. The fruiting display dominates the tree, although fruits are borne only on female trees. Birds like them.
Propagation: Seed.
Uses: *D. natalensis* makes a beautiful specimen. Growth is slow, about 30 cm per year under good conditions, where the summer is warm and rainfall high, even less under marginal conditions. However, this is not necessarily a disadvantage, for it means that the plant can be used in the tiniest garden. *D. natalensis* grows best in full sun, but tolerates partial shade. It is probably the finest of all indigenous bonsai trees.

Dombeya rotundifolia
Wild pear

Size: 3–8 x 3–8 m (wild), up to 6 x 5 m (garden)
Natural habitat: It is found over most of the east, in dry woodland, and may dominate rocky, north-facing hillsides.
Growth form: It is an upright tree with a rounded crown. Mature specimens have craggy, fissured bark. The leaves are circular and have the texture of sandpaper. In late autumn they first turn yellow at the edges, the yellow then spreading in fingers up between the veins. Finally, yellow turns to brown in the same pattern and sequence. The snow-white flowers appear in early spring when the tree is leafless, making a vivid splash against a veld gaunt from winter or blackened by fire. Bees love this tree.
Propagation: Seed, which must be collected as soon as the flower has dried out, before the central capsule splits.
Uses: *D. rotundifolia* is very reliable in the garden, never becoming excessively large. Growth is rapid, 1 m or more per year, and a pretty flowering specimen, worthy of a prime spot, results after three years. The ideal climate for this species is a hot summer with moderate rainfall, and a dry winter. However, this tree will tolerate high rainfall and a cool summer, although it does not flower as well under these conditions.

Why white? White flowers are generally pollinated by insects that have poor eyesight. However, these insects have a good sense of smell, so nearly all white flowers are scented. Nocturnal flowers, to which moths are attracted, tend to be white and are the most strongly scented of all.

Dombeya tiliacea
Forest dombeya

Size: 3–10 x 2–7 m (wild), up to 7 x 5 m (garden)
Natural habitat: This species occurs in the Eastern Cape and KwaZulu-Natal in evergreen forest and thick woodland, often on rocky hillsides.
Growth form: *D. tiliacea* is usually slender and upright, sometimes leaning on other trees. The leaves are heart-shaped. The flowers are white and delicate, produced in small, hanging clusters, and may cover the tree. Flowering takes place in autumn. Over winter, flowers turn russet and stay on the tree for months.
Propagation: Seed, which must be collected as soon as the flower has dried out, before the central capsule splits.
Uses: *D. tiliacea* is very fast growing in cultivation, reaching 4 m after three years, thickening out afterwards. First flowering occurs at about three years. It never becomes excessively large, so makes an ideal flowering specimen in almost every garden. It likes a warm summer with high rainfall, and has only slight frost tolerance.

Dovyalis longispina
Natal dovyalis

Size: 2–10 x 3–12 m (wild), up to 5 x 6 m (garden)
Natural habitat: *Dovyalis* is confined to the southeastern coastal plain. It occurs in lowland, dune and sand forests, rarely in open woodland.
Growth form: This is a ferociously spiny, shrubby tree. The spines are very long, slender and extremely sharp, which, combined with the stiffness of the branches, make the plant virtually impregnable. The foliage is attractive, the leaves being glossy and almost circular. *Dovyalis* is also noted for its fruiting displays. The fruits are the prettiest pale red plums, diffusely spotted with white. Birds love them. Only the female trees bear fruit.
Propagation: Seed, which must be fresh.
Uses: *Dovyalis* tends to retain its lower branches, so makes a wonderful hedge, although may be partially deciduous in a marginal climate. It is also ideal in a mixed bush clump in a bird garden. Speed of growth is about 60 cm per year. First fruiting occurs at around three years. The fruits have a sharp, refreshing flavour, and the few that escape the attention of the birds can be made into an exquisite jam. This tree likes a warm summer with moderate rainfall. Frost tolerance is unknown, but likely to be slight at best.

Cross-pollination *Dovyalis*, *Garcinia*, and *Ximenia* are amongst the many South African trees whose individual plants bear flowers of only one sex, nature's way of ensuring cross-pollination. When using these species it is advisable to plant at least three, to increase the chance of including both sexes, as young plants look alike.

Drypetes natalensis
Natal drypetes

Size: 3–10 x 3–10 m (wild), up to 6 x 6 m (garden)
Natural habitat: This is a species of the KwaZulu-Natal and Eastern Cape coasts. It is common in lowland forest, and also occurs in dune forest.
Growth form: *Drypetes* is often upright, but may be shrubby. It is noted for its attractive glossy foliage. The flowers are striking and always arouse comment. They are yellow and grow on the trunk and older branches. Although small, they are produced in such masses as to cover the bark, rather like an algal growth on rocks. The smell is musty, although scarcely unpleasant, as other books suggest. The velvety orange fruits erupt in bunches on the upper part of the main trunk. Only female trees bear fruit.
Propagation: Seed.
Uses: Although often found in semi-shade in its natural habitat, *Drypetes* grows best in full sun in the garden, and fruits much more prolifically in that position. With or without fruit, it makes a lovely small specimen. A typical growth rate is 30 cm per year. Fruiting begins at five years. *Drypetes* likes a warm summer with moderate to good rainfall. Drought tolerance is moderate and frost-hardiness unknown, but probably nil.

Ekebergia capensis
Cape ash, Dogplum, Essenhout

Size: 10–35 x 10–30 m (wild), up to 17 x 17 m (garden)
Natural habitat: This is a fairly common species, ranging from the Eastern Cape, through KwaZulu-Natal, to the far northeast. It occurs mainly in coastal and mist-belt forests, although sometimes forms the focus of a bush clump on a rocky outcrop in deciduous woodland.
Growth form: It is a beautiful tall tree, with a spreading canopy, and is evergreen over much of its range. However, it is briefly deciduous in a cold or dry winter, the leaves turning first yellow, then red just before they fall. It is also noted for its fruiting displays, which can be spectacular. The fruits are large, red and fleshy, and are a great favourite of hornbills and fruit bats. Only female trees bear fruit.
Propagation: Seed.
Uses: *Ekebergia* makes a good form and shade tree. The roots can be vigorous, lifting tarmac and paving. If this is not a problem it makes an ideal avenue or car-park tree. Speed of growth varies: where the summer is warm and wet 1 m per year is typical. Otherwise, growth is much slower. Under good conditions fruiting first occurs at about seven years. *Ekebergia* likes a temperate or warm summer with moderate to good rainfall, but tolerates some drought and slight frost.

Engineering for rain While a tree's leaves are positioned to maximise light reception, their pattern also conducts rainwater outwards, so that most of it will fall at the outer edge of the canopy. It is beneath this point that most of the tree's absorptive roots lie. Only heavy rain penetrates the central canopy.

Englerophytum magalismontanum
Stamvrug

Size: 2–6 x 5–8 m (wild), up to 3 x 4 m (garden)
Natural habitat: The stamvrug is found naturally in most of the northeast. It occurs at middle to high altitudes, always among rocks, and can dominate along cliff edges.
Growth form: This tree is always thickset. The leaves are very handsome and exhibit spectacular, even lurid, colour changes. New leaves are a satin-glossy golden-ginger. Then, as the leaves open, the upper-surfaces turn a delicate pale turquoise. Finally the under-surfaces turn white, while the upper-surfaces shed their hairs to reveal a polished, deep green. The whole colour scheme may be present on one twig. Honey-scented flowers cover the trunk and larger branches in spring. The fruits are bunched on older wood, and make a fine display. They are red, about 2 cm in diameter, and very tasty. Only female trees bear fruit.
Propagation: Seed.
Uses: The stamvrug looks its best when made the dominant feature in a steep, north-facing rockery. The fruits are loved by birds and the human manufacturers of exquisite jelly. Rate of growth is moderate, around 50 cm per year. Fruiting begins at about five years. The tree survives moderate frost, especially if backed by rocks. However, it dislikes the coastal climate.

Englerophytum natalense
Natal milkplum

Size: 3–8 x 2–5 m (wild), up to 6 x 4 m (garden)
Natural habitat: This species is found naturally on the coastal plain, from East London northwards. *E. natalense* is common in coastal lowland forest, either in the understorey or on the margins. It also occurs among rocks in steep kloofs.
Growth form: The growth form is upright and slender, and specimens growing unhindered in full sunshine have branches arranged in layers. The trunk of a mature tree becomes fluted at the base. The leaves are bi-coloured, green above, white below. The fruits are red, about 2 cm in diameter, and are eaten by birds and fruit bats. Only female trees bear fruit. This is the host plant of the butterflies *Pseudacraea lucretia* and *P. eurytus*.
Propagation: Seed – often planted by visiting birds.
Uses: *E. natalense* could be used as a specimen tree in a small garden, or to attract wildlife and fringe a forest clump on either the sunny or shady side of a large garden. It makes a good container plant that will grow well indoors, provided that the lighting is good. Growth rate is about 50 cm per year, with first fruiting at four years. *E. natalense* is frost-sensitive and grows best in high rainfall.

Seed dispersal Nature employs many couriers in its seed dispersal unit, and birds are one of the most important. Thus, bird-dispersed fruits need to advertise their readiness to be eaten, so the seed will be carried away from the parent. This is why the fruits are usually brightly coloured and highly visible.

Erythrina humeana
Dwarf coral tree

Size: 1–3 x 1–2 m (wild), up to 3 x 2 m (garden)
Natural habitat: This tree grows in grasslands and on the fringes of small bush clumps, ranging over much of the warmer parts of the east and southeast.
Growth form: It is a spindly little tree with few branches. The flowers appear in mid-summer. They are custom-built to attract birds, being red and tubular. Nectar collects in the bottom of the tubes ensuring that sunbirds, and other birds too, are in constant attendance. The flowers are borne in spikes and mature in sequence over an extended period, so that some are always in prime condition for the birds. The fruits are pretty too; they are cylindrical pods, which develop a beaded appearance as they hug the seeds within, splitting when mature to reveal the shining red-and-black seeds.
Propagation: Seed or cuttings.
Uses: *E. humeana* is the most useful of all *Erythrina* species in the garden. Its modest size permits it to be planted in the smallest garden and to be kept out of the frost against a sunny north-facing wall. It flowers and grows to its maximum size within two years, thereafter dying back slightly each winter, and making good the deficit in the following summer. It likes a warm summer with moderate rainfall.

Erythrina latissima
Broad-leaved coral tree

Size: 3–10 x 4–12 m (wild), up to 8 x 9 m (garden)
Natural habitat: *E. latissima* is found throughout much of the warmer parts of the east, typically on grassy hillsides and often among rocks. It seems equally at home on hot, dry, north-facing slopes and on cool, damp, south-facing slopes.
Growth form: It is a robust, heavily branched tree. Older specimens have corky bark. The leaves are huge and leathery. The flowers are custom-built to attract birds – deep red and tubular. The flowers appear in spring when the tree is leafless. Nectar collects in the bottom of the tubes ensuring that sunbirds, and other birds too, are in constant attendance. The flowers are borne in spikes and mature in sequence over an extended period, so that some are always in prime condition for the birds.
Propagation: Seed or cuttings.
Uses: This species grows well in cultivation, about 40–50 cm per year. Its pleasing shape and foliage make it a good specimen. It is an ideal bird tree and could be placed near the focal point of the garden. Flowers can first be expected at four years. It has vigorous roots and must be planted at least 4 m away from any wall. *E. latissima* likes a warm summer, but withstands some frost and fairly high rainfall.

Feeding birds with indigenous snacks Provide a fast-food outlet for nectar-loving birds by planting *Erythrina*, *Greyia*, *Halleria* and *Schotia*. You will offer a year-round snack bar for these delightful birds.

Erythrina lysistemon
Common coral tree

Size: 3–9 x 3–7 m (wild), up to 8 x 6 m (garden)
Natural habitat: This species is found in a variety of habitats throughout the warmer parts of the east and north.
Growth form: It is a fairly thickset tree. The flowers are red and tubular. Nectar collects in the bottom of the tubes ensuring that sunbirds are in constant attendance. The flowers are borne in spikes and mature in sequence over an extended period, so that some are always in prime condition for birds. Flowering begins in early spring when the tree is bare. Within a week the tree is brilliant red and besieged with nectar-feeders. The flowering peak lasts about a month, and pods containing beautiful red-and-black seeds follow.
Propagation: Seed and cuttings. Mature trees may suffer from boring insects. Cut off ailing branches below the infection.
Uses: Its fine performance in cultivation accounts for the widespread planting of this species, almost throughout the country. Growth is extremely fast, up to 1.5 m per year. After about three years vertical growth slows and the tree thickens out. Best flowering results where spring is dry and hot. The roots are vigorous – keep away from walls. *E. lysistemon* can cope with higher rainfall in hot areas with good drainage, or moderate temperatures if conditions are dry.

Euclea crispa
Blue guarri

Size: 3–6 x 3–5 m (wild), up to 5 x 4 m (garden)
Natural habitat: This tree is found naturally in most of South Africa, being absent only from the arid west and northern Lowveld. It occurs in open woodland, among rocks on grassy slopes, and especially on the margins of montane forest.
Growth form: *E. crispa* tends to be shrubby and even if single-stemmed always branches low down. It has grey bark that cracks into neat geometric squares. The leaves are very dark and slightly bluish; new spring growth is silvery white. The flowers are generally small, although pretty, providing short displays. Female trees bear berries that are initially red, black when mature, have a sweet taste and are an important source of food for birds. In a good season they cover the tree.
Propagation: Seed.
Uses: In cultivation *E. crispa* is a worker rather than a beauty. This tree makes a perfect screen and a nice addition to a bush or forest clump. In very barren areas it could be used to provide the initial shelter required by less tough species. *E. crispa* is useful in a bird garden. Growth rate is about 50 cm per year, and first flowering and fruiting occur at about four years. It thrives in all climates and even looks good throughout long droughts and the most severe frosts.

Root damage Roots can damage walls and paving. The best advice is never to plant a tree too close to a wall or swimming pool, and always leave a large circle open round any tree planted in a brick-paved area. For the big figs, leave up to 10 m between the tree and any wall; for *Erythrina*, 5 m; and for smaller trees, 2 m.

Euclea natalensis
Large-leaved guarri

Size: 3–12 x 3–9 m (wild), up to 8 x 7 m (garden)
Natural habitat: E. natalensis occupies the coastal strip from Port Elizabeth northwards, extending to the warmer parts of the east. It is common in dune forest and is also found in woodland and on koppies.
Growth form: This can be a tall, straight tree, but it is often small and spindly, and is frequently found growing in partial shade. Young trees have white bark, which becomes dark and craggily fissured with age. The leaves are an attractive, velvety yellow when new, dark when mature. The flowers are small and white, making a modest display in spring. The berries, which are borne only on female trees, have a sweet taste and are an important source of food for birds and bats. They are initially red, changing to black when mature. In a good season they cover the tree. This is the only Euclea that fruits well in partial shade.
Propagation: Seed.
Uses: E. natalensis makes a pleasant specimen, or can be used in a screen or forest clump. It is ideal in a bird garden. Growth rate is moderate, about 50 cm per year, and first flowering and fruiting occur at about four years. It likes a warm or temperate summer with moderate to good rainfall.

Euclea racemosa
Bush guarri

Size: 3–7 x 3–6 m (wild), up to 5 x 4 m (garden)
Natural habitat: E. racemosa ranges from the Eastern Cape through the warmer parts of KwaZulu-Natal to the far north-east. It is found in coastal and sand forests and is common in fairly dense, dry woodland.
Growth form: It is an upright tree with a dense, rounded crown. The leaves are thick and glossy, and the whole tree gleams in the sunshine. The flowers are white and pretty, and borne in sweet-smelling masses. Female trees bear berries that are initially red, black when mature, have a sweet taste and are an important source of food for birds. In a good season they cover the tree.
Propagation: Seed.
Uses: In cultivation, this makes a delightful specimen. As a young tree E. racemosa makes a screen; when mature, a small shade tree. It is ideal for a bird garden. Growth rate is moderate, about 50 cm per year, and first flowering and fruiting occur at about four years. E. racemosa likes moderate to high rainfall and a warm summer.

Flower arrangements Several indigenous trees have foliage that lasts well when cut, and can be used for flower arrangements. Try Euclea racemosa, Rhamnus prinoides, Rinorea angustifolia or Galpinia transvaalica.

Eugenia umtamvunensis
Pondo myrtle

Size: 4–10 x 4–10 m (wild), up to 5 x 5 m (garden)
Natural habitat: This is a very localised tree, being confined to the white sandstone soils near the Umtamvuna River in southern KwaZulu-Natal. It is found on forest edges.
Growth form: The growth form is upright, accentuated by the stiff, upswept look of the leaves. These are neat, glossy green above, almost white beneath, and exude a rich myrtle smell when crushed. The flowers are white and, although fairly small, they grow in masses, and so make a pleasing display. The fruits resemble small plums. These have a sweet-sour taste relished by people and birds alike.
Propagation: Seed, which must be fresh.
Uses: *E. umtamvunensis* is worth growing for its foliage alone and, because branches are retained at ground level, it also makes a good screen. It is a useful addition to a bird garden within the natural range, but fruiting is a bit erratic outside it. Initial growth is slow, accelerating after a couple of years, and producing a 2-m specimen at five years. *E. umtamvunensis* does not have to have sandy soil, growing just as well on shale. It likes a warm summer with at least moderate rainfall. Frost tolerance is slight.

Eugenia zuluensis
Wild myrtle

Size: 3–5 x 2–4 m (wild), up to 4 x 3 m (garden)
Natural habitat: *E. zuluensis* is confined to the east coast, from Port Elizabeth northwards, and to a few mist-belt forests in KwaZulu-Natal. It is usually found in the forest understorey where some sunlight filters through.
Growth form: *E. zuluensis* is a graceful small tree, often with a straight trunk. The bark has a flaking pattern, revealing patches of creamy underbark. The leaves are tiny, glossy and very attractive, and exude a rich myrtle smell when crushed. The flowers are white and, although fairly small, bloom in large enough masses to make a pleasing display. The fruits are bright red and can dominate the tree. These have a sweet-sour taste relished by people and birds alike.
Propagation: Seed, which must be fresh.
Uses: In cultivation *E. zuluensis* tends to be shrubby if grown in full sun. It then makes a good screen. To attain the shape seen in its natural habitat it must be pruned or grown in partial shade. Flowering begins at four years and is most prolific in full sun. *E. zuluensis* likes a warm or temperate climate with high or moderate rainfall and tolerates moderate frost. Speed of growth is about 40 cm per year.

Keep an eye on your sewer system Beware of planting trees, especially those known to have invasive root systems, over your sewerage outlet pipes. This can be a really costly business and plumbers are delighted by this sort of planting!

Euphorbia cooperi
Lesser candelabra tree

Size: 2–9 x 2–7 m (wild), up to 5 x 4 m (garden)
Natural habitat: It is found in the warm, dry parts of the east. It usually occurs on rocky north-facing slopes.
Growth form: *E. cooperi* has a straight trunk and succulent green branches, which grow in the shape of a candelabra. The oldest, lowest branches are constantly being shed, leaving the top branches to accentuate the candelabra form. The small flowers are a dull yellow. Although of modest beauty, they are much used by bees and other insects. The fruits are red capsules, quite attractive as they line up on the angled ridges of the branches. Small birds frequently nest in *E. cooperi*, and dead branches are easily excavated by hole-nesting birds. 
Propagation: Cuttings, details as for *E. ingens*.
Uses: *E. cooperi* can be used as a cactus substitute in rockeries, Mexican gardens or as a specimen. It is very effective when more than one tree is planted, spaced 3–6 m apart. Growth rate is about 60 cm per year. *E. cooperi* revels in the heat and grows best on a north-facing slope. It can cope with high rainfall provided that drainage is good.

Euphorbia ingens
Naboom

Size: 6–10 x 5–8 m (wild), up to 8 x 7 m (garden)
Natural habitat: It is widespread in the warmer parts of the east. It may form single-species stands on gentle north-facing slopes, or be regularly scattered in deciduous woodland.
Growth form: It is massively built when mature, with a thick trunk. The branches are green, leafless and grow in the shape of a candelabra, sweeping smoothly upwards. The result is a magnificent profile. The flowers are small and dull yellow, and much used by bees and other insects. The fruits are attractive, yellowish capsules. Dead branches are easily excavated by hole-nesting birds.
Propagation: Cuttings. Small cuttings are easiest to handle and make the best-shaped trees. The terminal 60–80 cm of a branch is ideal. The latex is unpleasant and a splash in the eye will be harmful. It is sensible to use gloves or sacking when handling these plants. Cuttings should be left to dry in a cool, shady spot for three days before planting.
Uses: *E. ingens* can be used as a cactus substitute in rockeries, Mexican gardens or as a specimen. Eventually, it makes an adequate shade tree. Growth rate is about 60 cm per year. It revels in the heat and grows best on a north-facing slope, but also tolerates occasional slight frost.

Euphorbia Cacti and *Euphorbia* are often confused and do bear some obvious resemblance to each other. However, cacti are American, while *Euphorbia* comes from Africa and Asia. Puncture a plant: if it exudes a clear watery liquid it is a cactus; if thick white latex oozes out, then it is *Euphorbia*.

Faurea saligna
Boekenhout

Size: 5–8 x 4–6 m (wild), up to 6 x 5 m (garden)
Natural habitat: *Faurea* is found in the warmer parts of the east, although absent from the Lowveld. It occurs in open woodland, often forming single-species stands.
Growth form: *Faurea* bears a superficial resemblance to a gum tree, and the bark is dark and ruggedly fissured. The leaves are thin, with red stalks, and quiver even in a gentle breeze. The tree is more or less evergreen, but turns a brilliant red in autumn, when many of the leaves are shed. This autumn flush begins at the top of the tree, and it then progresses downwards as the season advances. The flowers are white and catkin-like. *Faurea* is altogether a very beautiful tree, and a scattered stand on a rocky landscape is a fine sight.
Propagation: Seed, but germination rate is very poor. Cuttings have a reasonable strike rate. 
Uses: A single tree is well worth pride of place. Once it is established, *Faurea* grows 50 cm or more per year, provided that some soil from where it is found naturally is mixed into the planting hole: without it the growth rate is much slower. *Faurea* likes moderate rainfall and a warm summer.

Ficus abutilifolia
Large-leaved rock fig

Size: 2–8 x 3–10 m (wild), up to 5 x 6 m (garden)
Natural habitat: It occurs in the warm, rocky parts of the east and north, usually on a koppie or rock face.
Growth form: This is the prettiest fig. It is a rock-splitter, nearly always establishing among rocks and then outgrowing its crevices. The roots are great explorers, probing fissures, and flattening themselves into interesting shapes over smooth rocks. The leaves are large and heart-shaped. Ripe figs are red, and are eaten by birds such as parrots, louries, hornbills and green pigeons, as well as fruit bats, monkeys and antelopes.
Propagation: Cuttings, or a branch just stuck into the ground, may grow. Results are best if trimmed branches are planted in deep sand in August. Better-shaped trees are obtained from seed. It should be extracted from over-ripe or dried-out figs. *F. abutilifolia*'s seed is very fine and must be sown in a seed tray under glass to prevent its being blown away. 
Uses: This is a good rockery specimen in a hot, dry spot. It grows very straight for the first couple of years, spreading later. Growth rate is about 60 cm per year. Figs appear at eight years.

Planting time The ideal time to plant in summer rainfall areas is spring, as soon as the frost danger is past. This allows the longest possible time for the young plant to grow before the next winter sets in, bringing with it cold and drought.

Ficus glumosa
Mountain rock fig

Size: 5–9 x 8–18 m (wild), up to 7 x 12 m (garden)
Natural habitat: *F. glumosa* occurs in the hotter parts of the east, usually on a steep, rocky slope or a cliff edge.
Growth form: The main trunk is short but upright and the canopy wide-spreading. The bark has a nice yellow-grey flaking pattern. This is a rock-splitter. Its roots are large and mould themselves over surrounding rocks. The leaves bear fine yellow hairs that shimmer in the right light. The young growing points are completely enveloped in these hairs, the effect being complemented by orange stipules. The figs are fairly small and yellow, and clustered towards the ends of branches. Birds and bats love them.
Propagation: Cuttings and seed, details as for *F. abutilifolia*.
Uses: This species, and indeed any rock-splitter, can be planted in such a way as to simulate the tree's growth habit in the wild. Half bury two large rocks next to each other, with their flattest faces adjacent and parallel, forming a synthetic vertical fissure. Fill this with soil and plant the young fig on top of the fissure. Before the soil has eroded away, the fig roots will have reached true soil level, and will eventually fill the fissure and creep over the rocks. Growth rate is 40 cm per year. First fruiting occurs at about five years.

Ficus ingens
Red-leaved rock fig

Size: 5–9 x 8–20 m (wild), up to 7 x 15 m (garden)
Natural habitat: *F. ingens* is found in the east and the north, including areas that appear to experience heavy frost. It is always associated with koppies, cliff edges and rock outcrops in grassland, frequently on north-facing slopes.
Growth form: The growth form depends upon climate. Usually it is upright and spreading, casting good shade. However, in cold areas its 'height' may be less than 1 m, as it sculpts its canopy, often in a vertical plane, over a rock face, crouching out of the frost and maximising exposure to the sun. The tree's red spring leaf flush is a beautiful spectacle. It is best developed in a dry spring. Even in 'off' years the new leaves are an elegant bronze. The figs are small and yellow, and produced on the young branches. Birds and bats eat them.
Propagation: Cuttings and seed, details as for *F. abutilifolia*.
Uses: *F. ingens* makes a magnificent specimen, but needs space. Remember that the red spring flush will not develop if the tree receives extra water. Growth rate is about 50 cm per year and the canopy begins to spread at five years. First figs appear at three years. It can be cultivated in moderately frosty areas, but only if given a north-facing slope, preferably backed by flat rocks to store the winter sun's heat overnight.

Leaves at work The tree's workers, leaves, make the materials needed for plant growth. Carbon dioxide and water are the tree's raw materials. Photosynthesis is the process that converts these into sugar and cellulose, using sunlight as its energy source and chlorophyll as the agent that controls the process.

Ficus lutea
Giant-leaved fig

☼ 🌳 🍎 🐦 🦇 ☔

Size: 10–25 x 15–35 m (wild), up to 12 x 20 m (garden)
Natural habitat: *F. lutea* occurs naturally in coastal lowland forest in KwaZulu-Natal.
Growth form: It is large, with a neatly flat-topped canopy, often twice as wide as the tree is tall. It can be a strangler, a lifestyle every bit as sinister as it sounds. Instead of germinating on the ground, a young fig germinates in a pocket of leaf litter in the fork of a tree. It grows happily in this position by sending roots down to the soil. It has taken a great short cut to the sunshine in the process, and eventually overwhelms its host, although may take a century to engulf it completely. *F. lutea* has enormous leaves, epitomising tropical bounty. The figs are yellow and fairly small, and borne on terminal branches – birds and bats like them. Birds often nest in rotting knot-holes, in dead branches.
Propagation: Cuttings and seed, details as for *F. abutilifolia*.
Uses: Despite its quite considerable size, *F. lutea* is widely cultivated, notably in the Durban area, as an avenue tree. It is certainly a worthy subject, the combination of shape and leaf size being unique. Growth is rapid, at least 1.3 m per year when young, and it makes an acceptable shade tree after four years. It likes good rainfall.

Ficus natalensis
Natal fig

☼ 🌳 🍎 🐦 🦇 ☔

Size: 10–18 x 16–32 m (wild), up to 12 x 22 m (garden)
Natural habitat: *F. natalensis* occurs in coastal lowland forest and sometimes as an isolated specimen among rocks in grassland in the warm eastern interior.
Growth form: It is large and spreading, casting dense shade. The trunk is massive and has great character. It sprouts aerial roots, and in time these thicken and may fuse with the main trunk. Individuals that began life as stranglers develop the strangest contortions of the trunk as they strive, unsuccessfully, to cover up their strangling past. The figs are small and yellow, and masses grow on young branches.
Propagation: Cuttings and seed, details as for *F. abutilifolia*.
Uses: *F. natalensis* should only be used in a large garden, as its shade will limit the growth of any near neighbours. The strangling habit can be induced by planting a very small seedling in potting mixture in the fork of an expendable victim. As it outgrows its substrate the young fig will send a root down to the soil and progress as in the wild. It fruits reliably and heavily, and the sheer size of the tree makes it a perfect roost. Growth is initially about 1.3 m per year. Later upward growth slows as spread accelerates. Fruiting begins at three years. *F. natalensis* likes high rainfall. It is a favourite bonsai.

Bird gardens The first garden of all was a bird garden. Brueghel's picture of the Garden of Eden shows an informal parkland full of birds. The only contact that many people have with birds and other wildlife is in their garden. Plant trees that attract birds, such as *Acacia*, *Erythrina* and *Ficus*.

Ficus sansibarica
Zanzibar fig

Size: 8–12 x 11–16 m (wild), up to 8 x 10 m (garden)
Natural habitat: This species' natural habitat is confined, in South Africa, to the Lowveld.
Growth form: This is a fine, spreading tree, typically wider than it is tall. *F. sansibarica* can be a strangler, and even free-growing specimens have prominent above-ground root systems that envelop boulders and walls. It is virtually evergreen, thinning briefly in a dry winter. The fruiting display is spectacular; the figs are large and a rich reddish-purple, and erupt directly from the trunk and larger branches. As with all figs, the 'fruit' is in reality a series of flowers enclosed in the receptacle. A whole miniature ecosystem exists inside the fig, with small wasps pollinating the flowers, and they themselves being parasitised by another type of wasp. The little brown pips inside the mature fig are the true fruits.
Propagation: Cuttings and seed, details as for *F. abutilifolia*.
Uses: *F. sansibarica* makes a fine specimen. The roots are exceptionally vigorous, even by fig standards. Like all figs, it is best planted away from buildings and paving. Growth rate is about 60 cm per year. A lovely shade tree results after six years or so. Fruiting has first been observed, outside the natural range, at nine years.

Ficus sur
Cape fig

Size: 10–15 x 12–18 m (wild), up to 12 x 15 m (garden)
Natural habitat: *F. sur* occurs in coastal regions in the south and east, extending inland to the far northeast. It grows on rocky outcrops, in forest, and swampy areas, often growing barely above the water table.
Growth form: It is tall and spreading. The trunk is smooth and almost white, and specimens growing on the edges of swamps or rivers have buttresses at the base of the trunk. Autumn leaves can be showy, but the spring flush is often spectacular, new leaves being brilliant red, changing to bronze and finally green. *F. sur*'s figs are the finest of all. They are 3 cm and more in diameter and red, growing in large bunches sprouting from the trunk or main branches. Fruiting branches are retained after the figs have fallen, giving old trees a shaggy appearance.
Propagation: Seed, which should be extracted from over-ripe or dried-out figs. It is very fine and must be sown in a seed tray under glass to prevent it being blown away.
Uses: *F. sur* is an excellent shade tree and a magnet for birds and bats when the fruits are ripe. It will thrive in a boggy spot provided that some of the roots are not in waterlogged soil. Growth rate is 2 m per year initially, and fruiting commences at two years. It tolerates slight frost.

Autumn leaves Autumn colours are strictly functional. As a tree enters the dry season, it discards its main evaporative surface, its foliage. But first it retrieves precious chlorophyll from the leaves. Then the coloured waste products and other leaf pigments have their moment of red or yellow glory.

Ficus sycomorus
Sycamore fig

Size: 10–25 x 18–50 m (wild), up to 14 x 25 m (garden)
Natural habitat: This species is confined to the Lowveld and the north coast of KwaZulu-Natal. It grows beside rivers and on seasonal floodplains.
Growth form: This is South Africa's largest fig tree. A walk among these giants in the fig forest in Mkuzi Game Reserve is a memorable experience. The trunk is pale yellow. It is buttressed towards the base, and the buttresses fork and twist, providing hiding places for small animals. The figs are large and red, and borne in branches on the main trunk and older branches. The whole tree may be covered in figs, but more often the branches 'take turns' to fruit, so that the tree may bear fruit all year round. This strategy ensures that it retains the attention of large fruit-eating birds permanently. The canopy thins a little in winter.
Propagation: Cuttings and seed, details as for *F. abutilifolia*.
Uses: This tree is the sycamore of the Bible and was used as a shade and avenue tree in ancient Egypt. *F. sycomorus* is suitable only for a very large garden. It grows about 1.4 m per year, and starts spreading at four years. First figs are produced at five years, even outside the natural range. *F. sycomorus* is always full of birds.

Ficus tremula
Quiver-leaf fig

Size: 2–6 x 1–4 m (wild), up to 4 x 3 m (garden)
Natural habitat: *F. tremula* is a localised species, being confined to northern Zululand. The tree occurs in forests, particularly in sand forest.
Growth form: It can grow as a normal tree but is most often a mild strangler (technically it is a strangler, but is too small and feeble to do any damage) or epiphyte – merely using its host as a perch. The growth form is always upright and delicate and it never overwhelms its host. The leaves are glossy and thin, and tremble in the wind. The figs are small and grow evenly scattered over the whole of the trunk and large branches. They are green, even when mature, and are a favourite with birds.
Propagation: Cuttings and seed, details as for *F. abutilifolia*.
Uses: *F. tremula* is the only small, neat, indigenous fig and makes a sensational garden subject, provided that the summer is warm and rainfall moderate to high. Although very frost-sensitive, it is small enough to grow against a north-facing shelter – its roots being too small to cause damage. Growth rate is about 80 cm per year. First fruiting occurs at about three years. It makes an excellent bonsai subject.

Make an indigenous bonsai Many indigenous trees make marvellous bonsai subjects. Seedlings can be collected in the veld and trained into these delightful miniature specimens. Several indigenous species do well as bonsais: *Olea europaea* and *Celtis africana* are favourites, and most species of *Ficus* and *Commiphora* work wonderfully.

Ficus trichopoda
Hippo fig, Swamp fig

Size: 7–12 x 8–15 m (wild), up to 8 x 11 m (garden)
Natural habitat: *F. trichopoda* is confined to swamp forests on the coastal plain, north of Durban.
Growth form: Of all local figs, this species looks most like the popular image of a tropical fig. The trunk is very smooth and puts out large stilt roots, as do the lower branches. These develop into satellite trunks and may become the main means of support, as with the Indian banyan tree. Branches are tipped bright red. The huge, glossy leaves have neat herringbone veins. The figs are red and quite large, growing on the young branches.
Propagation: Cuttings and seed, details as for *F. abutilifolia*. The best way to root cuttings is to completely bury metre-long sections of branch horizontally, in a few centimetres of soil.
Uses: *F. trichopoda* makes a striking specimen, as well as a good shade tree. Despite its dependence upon swampy conditions in the wild, *F. trichopoda* thrives in an ordinary warm garden. It enjoys a boggy spot, but high rainfall suits it just as well. The first aerial roots appear at two years and they root in the soil at four years.

Galpinia transvaalica
Wild pride-of-India

Size: 4–15 x 5–15 m (wild), up to 9 x 10 m (garden)
Natural habitat: *Galpinia* is an endemic with a narrow distribution, extending from the Lowveld to northern Zululand. It is most frequently a component of deciduous woodland, although is sometimes found in evergreen forest near rivers, where it grows to its greatest size.
Growth form: *Galpinia* is a thickset tree that branches low down. The leaves are glossy, with a waxy bloom. The spring flush is red. The flowers are white and, although small, bloom in dense heads that cover the tree in mid-summer. The flowers are a great favourite with butterflies. The fruit resembles a red-brown berry but is dry, and when squeezed is found to be a pack of flattened seeds ready for wind-dispersal.
Propagation: Seed.
Uses: *Galpinia* is worth growing for its flowers or as a foliage specimen. First flowering has been noted at two years, but more typically takes place at about six years. Cut foliage retains its beauty for many days in a flower arrangement. Growth rate is about 80 cm per year. *Galpinia* looks its best when grown where the summer is warm and the winter dry. It tolerates light frosts.

When to stake Wait until the trunk of your tree is sturdy enough to withstand the wind before removing the lower branches. Let staking be a last resort. Staking is usually only necessary when a tree has been badly planted, or pruned too soon. In extremely windy areas, choose trees that naturally cope with these conditions.

Garcinia livingstonei
African mangosteen

Size: 2–8 x 2–12 m (wild), up to 5 x 6 m (garden)
Natural habitat: *G. livingstonei* is locally common in parts of the eastern Lowveld and northern Zululand. It occurs in a variety of habitats, growing to its largest size in sand forest.
Growth form: The young tree's branches grow horizontally in layers, regularly spaced vertically. Older, lower layers are widest, so the tree takes on a pyramidal shape. Later in life the lower branches are lost, leaving a heavy, stiff crown. The leaves are thickly leathery and bluish in colour. Flowers grow along the branches; male flowers, with their powder-puff bunches of stamens, are very showy and sweet-smelling. The fruits are large orange plums, delicious, and sweeter to the human palate than most wild fruits. Only female trees bear fruit. 
Propagation: Seed.
Uses: Flowering and fruiting are a bit unpredictable, although fruiting has been noted at four years in cultivation. Nevertheless, *Garcinia* will always make an unusual and good-looking specimen by virtue of its foliage and shape alone. Growth rate is about 30 cm per year.

Gardenia thunbergia
White gardenia

Size: 3–5 x 3–5 m (wild), up to 4 x 4 m (garden)
Natural habitat: This is a coastal and mist-belt species, ranging from Port Elizabeth to northern Zululand. It occurs in evergreen forest, usually in the shady interior.
Growth form: It is a small, stout tree with a distinctive, right-angled branching pattern. The flowers are large, pure white trumpets, and sweet-smelling. The fruits are tough and grey-green, and the size and shape of hen's eggs. Apparently unappetising, they are eaten by large mammals after they have fallen.
Propagation: Seed, which is best collected from the over-ripe fruit once it has fallen.
Uses: *G. thunbergia* develops its typical shape at an early age, so makes a characterful specimen suitable for a small garden. It grows well in almost any climate and is even used on road verges in Johannesburg. It thrives and flowers in semi-shade. Growth rate is about 30 cm per year, but flowering and fruiting, even outside the natural range, begin at three years.

Bees and ultraviolet Anthocyanin pigments create a blue colour in flowers when the cell sap is alkaline. Blue flowers are pollinated primarily by bees, which can see ultraviolet light that is imperceptible to the human eye. Flowers that look uniform blue to us are often streaked with ultraviolet, to guide bees to pollen.

Gardenia volkensii
Transvaal gardenia

Size: 3–6 x 3–7 m (wild), up to 4 x 4 m (garden)
Natural habitat: *G. volkensii* is found in Zululand and much of the northeast. It occurs in dry woodland.
Growth form: It is very chunky in build, older specimens having a thick trunk and a solid mass of branches. The leaves are quite pretty, long and thin, waxy, and dark green in colour. The flowers are large and pure white, and sweetly scented. The fruit is egg-shaped and up to 8 cm long. It has a ribbed surface and is pale grey in colour. Fruits persist on the tree for months. Antelopes and warthogs eat them after they have fallen, and disperse seeds in their droppings.
Propagation: Seed, which is best collected from the over-ripe fruit once it has fallen.
Uses: This species has been widely used in cultivation and deservedly so. The growth rate is about 30 cm per year, but *G. volkensii* always looks its best, however small. At about four years, flowering begins and fruiting takes place outside the native range. If cut when ripe, the fruits can be used in dried flower arrangements and last for years. *G. volkensii* likes a temperate to warm summer, with moderate rainfall.

Gonioma kamassi
Kamassi

Size: 2–6 x 2–5 m (wild), up to 4 x 3 m (garden)
Natural habitat: *Gonioma* is virtually endemic to the south of the country, where it occurs in evergreen forest in the shady understorey.
Growth form: It is a small, delicate tree. Its slender shape is emphasised by the upswept leaves. These are exceptionally clean-cut and glossy, and arranged, almost uniquely among South African trees, in groups of four. This arrangement conveys the pleasing impression of repetitive symmetry, normally the preserve of compound-leaved trees. *Gonioma* has pretty, white and waxy flowers, which are sweetly scented and borne in small bunches.
Propagation: Seed.
Uses: Although happy in the shade, *Gonioma* thrives in sunshine. In full sun it may flower at one year, before it is knee-high. Even without flowers it is a charming form and foliage plant, suitable for smaller gardens. The tree's growth rate is moderate, about 50 cm per year. *Gonioma* enjoys a temperate or warm climate, with high rainfall. Its performance in frost or drought is unknown.

Seeds and fruits Seeds and fruits are relatively modern developments. Early plants reproduced and dispersed by means of spores. These are easily spread by wind but carry only a tiny food resource and are easily killed by desiccation. Seeds, however, contain substantial food reserves and resist drought.

Grewia hexamita
Giant raisin

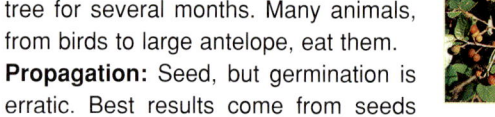

Size: 3–6 x 3–6 m (wild), up to 4 x 4 m (garden)
Natural habitat: It is found in the Lowveld and Zululand, occurring in open grassy areas and in sparse, dry woodland.
Growth form: It is normally a tree with a graceful weeping habit. The leaves are large, and grow in an overlapping zig-zag in the same plane. They are shiny green above, pure white below, and flash silver in the wind. New growth is red. The flowers are yellow and 5 cm in diameter, and make a fine show. The fruits are dull orange and have a thin, dry, but edible flesh. They remain on the tree for several months. Many animals, from birds to large antelope, eat them. 
Propagation: Seed, but germination is erratic. Best results come from seeds collected from warthog and baboon droppings. Presumably it is their stomach acids that help dissolve the tough seed coat.
Uses: *Grewia* makes a good screen, although in marginal climates it is semi-deciduous. It is essential in bush clumps or a bird garden. Initial growth is 1 m or more per year, subsequently slowing as the plant thickens out. Flowering and fruiting commence in the second year.

Greyia sutherlandii
Natal bottlebrush

Size: 2–6 x 2–5 m (wild), up to 3 x 3 m (garden)
Natural habitat: *Greyia* is found over much of KwaZulu-Natal, extending into adjacent uplands in the other provinces. It always occurs on rocky hillsides or cliff edges.
Growth form: It is a small, craggy tree that branches low down. The trunk tends to be twisted and furrowed, the bark shaggy. The leaves are large and attractive. The rich green of summer turns yellow and red, spotted with black, in autumn. In spring, *Greyia* is covered in large red bottlebrush flowers that produce copious nectar, attracting sunbirds and sugarbirds.
Propagation: Seed, although cuttings strike well.
Uses: *Greyia* is well worth growing for its flowers and its bird-attracting qualities. This is an ideal tree where the climate is temperate to cool and the rainfall moderate to high. It struggles in a hot summer. It is also fairly sensitive to frost, despite occurring naturally in very cold areas. Wild specimens are often partially sheltered, or grow on steep north-facing slopes. The tree's growth is fairly rapid, about 80 cm per year initially, and first flowering can be expected at three years.

Weeping trees Trees of weeping form are traditionally placed near water, a practice which originated with the occurrence of weeping willows alongside European rivers. It so happens that all indigenous weeping trees grow well, and look appropriate, beside water, even if some are found naturally in drier habitats.

Gymnosporia buxifolia
Common spike-thorn, Pendoring

Size: 2–5 x 2–4 m (wild), up to 3 x 3 m (garden)
Natural habitat: This is one of South Africa's most common and widespread trees, being absent only from the far west of the country. It occurs in most habitats. 
Growth form: Most often it is a craggy little tree, bristling with spines. The bark is deeply fissured and ridged. The leaves are usually more or less grey, or even bluish. The flowers are small and white but grow in masses. They have a musty, but not unpleasant, smell, and are a favourite of bees and other insects. Flowering may be so profuse that the outline of the branches and even the shape of the whole tree is obscured. The fruit is a small dull-coloured capsule which splits into three when mature, revealing orange or red seeds that attract birds.
Propagation: Seed.
Uses: It makes an impenetrable barrier and has rugged charm. The bluish leaves add variation to foliage texture. *Gymnosporia* flowers at about three years and is worth growing for its value to wildlife. Growth rate is modest, around 50 cm per year. This is one of the toughest of all trees.

Halleria lucida
Tree fuchsia, Notsung

Size: 3–8 x 4–10 m (wild), up to 5 x 6 m (garden)
Natural habitat: *Halleria* is found in all the wetter regions, from the Western Cape to the far northeast. It is especially common in mist-belt forest, but occurs in many other habitats too, often among rocks.
Growth form: Very variable. When exposed to frost and marginal rainfall in the open, a small round shrub results; in forest, tall, straight-trunked trees can be found. *Halleria* is evergreen, thinning a little in a harsh winter. Its flowers are curved orange tubes, which grow in bunches all over the main trunk and larger branches. Sunbirds flock to them. The fruits are berry-like, initially green, maturing to black. They are sought by white-eyes and other small fruit-eaters, including fruit bats.
Propagation: Seed. Layering is another option.
Uses: *Halleria* is worth growing for its flowers and is ideal in a bird garden. A good way to enjoy *Halleria* is to plant it on the edge of a terrace, above a favourite sitting place. In this way it provides shade, and the visiting birds can easily be watched from underneath. Flowering begins at two years and is almost continuous from four years onwards. Garden specimens are always multi-stemmed and make a good, if rambling, hedge. Growth rate is 1 m per year in a temperate, wet climate.

Layering Propagating plants by means of layering can be encouraged by pinning a low, hanging branch down on the ground with a heavy stone. Once roots have formed on this branch, that section of the branch can be cut off and treated in the same way as a rooted cutting.

Heteromorpha trifoliata
Parsley tree, Parsnip tree

Size: 3–8 x 2–5 m (wild), up to 7 x 4 m (garden)
Natural habitat: *Heteromorpha* is found throughout South Africa, except in the arid regions. It occurs in many habitats and climates, ranging from moist, evergreen forest to hot, dry woodland and high altitude grassland.
Growth form: It is always slender in form, even when multi-stemmed. The bark is unique and most attractive: shiny and copper-coloured, not unlike some *Commiphora* species, but is regularly marked with horizontal bands. A fissure develops at each band and the bark peels from this point. Intensity of bark colour and peel is best developed in warm, dry climates. The tree has highly diverse leaf forms, hence the name, and a crushed leaf smells pleasantly of parsley. The fruits are tiny, dry, sculpted structures, which grow in spherical heads. 
Propagation: Seed.
Uses: *Heteromorpha* is a must for bark enthusiasts and can be used as an accent plant in the same way as its relatives, the cabbage trees. The growth rate, even in dry areas, is rapid, often 2 m and more per year initially.

Heteropyxis natalensis
Lavender tree

Size: 3–8 x 2–5 m (wild), up to 6 x 4 m (garden)
Natural habitat: *Heteropyxis* is found naturally in the warmer parts of the east. It occurs in forest, usually on the margins, but is more typical of rocky outcrops in woodland and grassland, and especially on cliff edges.
Growth form: It is a slender, upright tree. The bark is white and smooth on young trees, but turns grey with age, gradually flaking to reveal patches of pale orange-brown underbark. The leaves are glossy, with a waxy texture. In spring, new growth flushes red, and in autumn there is an extended display of yellow and deep orange. However, the smell of the foliage is its most attractive feature. A crushed leaf has a strong, sweet lavender smell, as rich and pleasing as the famous herb.
Propagation: Seed, which is as fine as dust, so must be germinated beneath glass to avoid its being blown away.
Uses: *Heteropyxis* is the ideal small specimen tree and deserves a prime position. If planted next to a stoep, it will be an endless source of entertainment to visitors, who can never resist pinching the leaves. Growth is rapid, about 80 cm per year. *Heteropyxis* thrives in high or low rainfall. However, the spring and autumn colours develop best in dry areas. It makes a good bonsai.

Planting a grove A grove of same-species trees makes a lovely feature. Plant five or seven *Heteropyxis natalensis* in a loose triangle and create your own copse. *Acacia nigrescens* or *Acacia xanthophloea*, *Canthium mundianum*, and *Spirostachys* will also look good in an arrangement like this.

Hippobromus pauciflorus
Basterperdepis

Size: 3–5 x 3–4 m (wild), up to 4 x 3 m (garden)
Natural habitat: *Hippobromus* is found in much of the south and east of the country. It occurs in virtually every habitat, although looks its best in fairly dense, deciduous woodland.
Growth form: It is a small tree, but may also be a multi-stemmed upright shrub. The leaves are divided into toothed leaflets, and are most attractive. They bear a supposed resemblance to those of the real 'perdepis' ('horse piss' – the common name of *Clausena*) but have no scent. One story goes that the name *Hippobromus* ('horse-stench') was intended for perdepis, but that the dried (and scentless) specimens were mixed up when the scientific names were originally assigned. The tree's flowers are small and white, and make a brief but showy display, which is well attended by insects, in mid-winter.
Propagation: Seed, although this is hard to find. It may be more practical to find a tiny seedling beneath a parent plant.
Uses: *Hippobromus* makes a pleasant foliage specimen and its dense foliage can also be used in a screen. Soil disturbance around the roots induces suckering, producing a little thicket. Growth is fairly fast, about 70 cm per year. *Hippobromus* enjoys most climates.

Hymenocardia ulmoides
Red heart

Size: 3–7 x 3–7 m (wild), up to 4 x 4 m (garden)
Natural habitat: *Hymenocardia* is found in Zululand and the Lowveld. It occurs in coastal lowland forest but is most common in sand forest, notably in Mkuzi Game Reserve.
Growth form: It may be shrubby, but can grow into an upright tree. It is more or less evergreen and has tiny neat leaves, all produced in the same plane on one branch. New growth is pink, and older leaves turn a beautiful spangled red before they fall. The flowers are single-sexed and most intriguing. Male flowers are minute pink bobbles arranged in vertical spikes; female flowers are greenish-yellow, with thin protruding red styles. The fruits are borne only on female trees and are exceptionally pretty – they are small and pink, consisting of papery, winged structures, which hang in bunches.
Propagation: Seed, which must be collected before it turns brown and falls from the parent tree. Parasites often attack after this stage.
Uses: *Hymenocardia* is worth growing as a fruiting specimen or for its foliage alone. First fruiting occurs at six years, even outside the natural range. Speed of growth is about 40 cm per year, provided the summer is warm and rainfall good.

A bushveld garden The simplest natural garden to create is a 'bushveld' garden – with open areas, clumps of bushes and small trees, and a few big trees. It will attract garden birds, as most are bushveld species. Use plants suited to your climate and soil conditions. Plants' sizes and how you arrange them are also important factors in planning your garden.

Hyphaene coriacea
Ilala palm

Size: 2–6 x 3–8 m (wild), up to 3 x 5 m (garden)
Natural habitat: *Hyphaene* is restricted to the eastern lowlands, where it ranges from the Eastern Cape to the far northeast. It usually occurs in sandy grasslands.
Growth form: Several trunks arch outwards, each topped with a mop of large, fan-shaped, blue-grey leaves. The fruits, which grow in huge bunches on female trees, take two years to develop and are large, rounded, and orange. The outer layer is edible and sweet, and a favourite food of elephants, the main dispersal agents. Mature fruits hang on the tree for up to two years and make good permanent dried ornaments.
Propagation: Seed. This germinates well enough, if slowly, provided that fruits are collected when the outer layer is still soft. Sometimes fallen fruits can be found with roots just emerging. Plant the seed either directly into the ground or into tall thin packets. When planting a packeted plant it is important to cut off the base of the packet carefully, place the plant in position, slit the side of the packet and fill up the planting hole. This ensures minimum root disturbance.
Uses: *Hyphaene* makes a beautiful specimen. Rate of growth is about 30 cm per year. Fruiting begins at 10 years. It likes sandy soil and a warm summer, with moderate to good rainfall.

Ilex mitis
Cape holly

Size: 7–20 x 7–17 m (wild), up to 10 x 10 m (garden)
Natural habitat: *Ilex* is a widespread species, extending throughout the wetter part of the country from the south-western Cape to the far northeast. It is found in evergreen forest, nearly always next to a stream.
Growth form: *Ilex* is a tall tree, with smooth, almost white bark in early maturity. Older trees develop great gnarls and outgrowths, and can become characters worthy of a Tolkien epic. Silvery young twigs make a pleasing contrast with the pink leaf stalks. The leaves are deep green and make a dense canopy. The flowers are insignificant, but, in autumn and early winter, female trees bear heavy crops of small red berries, greatly loved by birds.
Propagation: Seed.
Uses: *Ilex* is worth growing as a form specimen and to provide shade. Specimens grown in full sun tend to be bushy and a little trimming is needed to make a good shade tree. Fruiting cannot be guaranteed because young seedlings cannot be sexed, and much love and energy might be invested in a fruitless male. *Ilex* likes a temperate summer with good rainfall. In a winter rainfall area, a high water table will achieve the same effect. Growth is rapid, about 80 cm per year.

Avoiding termites Don't make pyramids of soil around the base of your trees. This encourages termites and covers up the breathing pores on the trunk. A tree's roots should be covered with soil and its trunk should be above ground.

Inhambanella henriquesii
Inhambanella

Size: 10–18 x 13–30 m (wild), up to 12 x 15 m (garden)
Natural habitat: *Inhambanella* is found in Zululand, where it occurs on the margins of swamp forest, on the lee side of dune forest and as a component of forest copses in grassland.
Growth form: It is a massive evergreen tree with a dense crown. The foliage is remarkable for its new growth, which appears in fiery red bursts at any time of the year. The flowers are quite a pretty yellow, but largely hidden beneath the foliage. The fruits are large and orange, and most attractive.
Propagation: Seed.
Uses: *Inhambanella* is ideal where deep, cool shade is required, provided that enough space is available. It grows best where rainfall is good or the water table high. It might be the only big tree that will grow in a really waterlogged spot. Flowering and fruiting begin at about 20 years. Initial growth rate is about 50 cm per year, slowing later as the tree thickens and develops its spreading crown.

Kigelia africana
Sausage tree

Size: 8–15 x 10–30 m (wild), up to 10 x 18 m (garden)
Natural habitat: This species occurs naturally in the Lowveld and Zululand, where it is usually found beside rivers and pans.
Growth form: *Kigelia* is a big, impressive tree, and it has a spreading canopy. The flowers are spectacular, large, and intense dark maroon. They bloom in dangling strings beneath the canopy, allowing bat pollinators access. Sunbirds also visit the flowers, but 'steal' the nectar through punctures, bypassing the pollination route. Mature flowers carpet the ground after falling, and are eaten by grey duikers. The fruits are even more bizarre – giant wooden sausages, up to 80 cm long, which hang from the tree for several months. Elephants and other large mammals act as dispersal agents.
Propagation: Seed or cuttings.
Uses: Growth rate is at least 1 m per year, which makes it a good shade tree, but beware falling sausages. First flowering takes place at about six years, with sausages produced soon afterwards. Both flowering and fruiting take place well outside the natural range, provided that the tree stands in open space. If cramped, it flowers less well and there will be few or no fruits. Sausage trees thrive in warm summers, wet or dry, but may be leafless during a cold, dry winter.

Decorative pods Large woody fruits are dispersed by mammals, but are usually only eaten after they fall to the ground, and so they decorate the tree for some time. If picked when fully ripe, these fruits, and also dried pods and winged *Combretum* seeds, make lovely displays in baskets and wooden bowls.

Kiggelaria africana
Wild peach

Size: 6–15 x 5–13 m (wild), up to 9 x 8 m (garden)
Natural habitat: The wild peach is found in nearly all the wetter parts of South Africa, most commonly in the mist-belt forest of KwaZulu-Natal. It also occurs alongside rivers in Cape fynbos and on koppies in cool damp grassland.
Growth form: It is a grey-green, upright tree, exceptionally attractive to birds. The fruits are small green capsules, the seeds inside ripening unobserved. When the outer case splits, it reveals brilliant orange seeds. This is the moment the birds have been waiting for, making it difficult to find exposed ripe seeds in the wild. The wild peach has one other big attraction for birds. It is the host of the butterflies *Cymothoe alcimeda* and *Acraea horta*. The latter has small black caterpillars that occasionally festoon the tree, to the delight of cuckoos.
Propagation: Seed, often planted by birds in flowerbeds.
Uses: This species is ideal for a bird garden. Flowering and fruiting commence at two years, but note that only female trees bear fruit. The small black caterpillars may defoliate a young tree if the cuckoos fail to find them. This is not a problem, as the caterpillars will disappear anyway and the tree will grow a new set of leaves. Given high rainfall growth is rapid, about 1 m per year.

Kirkia acuminata
White syringa

Size: 8–15 x 8–15 m (wild), up to 12 x 12 m (garden)
Natural habitat: *Kirkia* occurs naturally in the warm, dry woodlands of the far northeast.
Growth form: This is an upright tree, thin when young, with branches arranged in a neat series of layers. The tree develops a fine spreading canopy when mature. The bark of young trees is pale grey and shiny, and the trunks gleam brilliantly in low-angled winter sunshine when the leaves have fallen. In some areas, the bark of older trees becomes fissured. The leaves display a wonderful range of colours. The fresh glossy green of summer contrasts with the red leaf stalks. As autumn approaches, the leaves turn yellow or red. The reds deepen in cold weather, until the leaves are almost black. Not all the leaves change at once, so the bright colours last almost until spring.
Propagation: Seed or cuttings.
Uses: *Kirkia* is recommended as a feature tree and is compulsory for admirers of autumn colours. In cultivation the characteristic bark fissures develop at the base of the trunk at three years, extending upwards later. Growth is very fast, initially at least 1 m per year, if the summer is warm. *Kirkia* likes moderate rainfall, but cannot stand frost.

Ripe or unripe? For best germination results, collect wild fruit or berries as they ripen. But, from trees such as *Kiggelaria* or *Turraea*, you may have to take unripe fruit, before the birds eat it. You have to guess, or test by breaking open a sample to see if the inside has turned orange. A day or so after this the fruit splits naturally and birds get the lot.

Lagynias lasiantha
Natal medlar

Size: 3–5 x 3–5 m (wild), up to 3 x 3 m (garden)
Natural habitat: *Lagynias* is confined to lowland KwaZulu-Natal and to a small area in the far northeast. It is found in a variety of forest types, most often along the margins.
Growth form: It is a small tree with a slight tendency to scramble if crowded. The branching pattern, at least in the young plant, is very precise: branches are in exactly opposite pairs, each pair being at right angles to the pairs above and below it. *Lagynias* has small cream flowers that yellow with age. They are bunched at the bases of the leaf stalks and make a modest display. The fruits are brilliant, glossy green spheres that mature to a rich orange-brown. The ripe fruit is delicious and much loved by all animals.
Propagation: Seed, but germination is erratic, perhaps due to the presence or absence of vital soil micro-organisms. Try including soil from the tree's natural range in the nursery mix.
Uses: *Lagynias* makes an unusual and interesting garden specimen and can also be used in a mixed screen or thicket. First fruiting takes place, within the natural range, at only two years. Outside its natural range there are no guarantees – bird gardeners take note. Growth rate is about 50 cm per year. *Lagynias* likes good rainfall, but tolerates some drought.

Leucosidea sericea
Ouhout

Size: 3–8 x 4–12 m (wild), up to 4 x 6 m (garden)
Natural habitat: *Leucosidea* is found in the cool Highveld areas of the eastern half of the country. It is very common alongside streams or on forest margins.
Growth form: It is evergreen and can be an erect tree with a good canopy, but usually branches low down. The bark is shaggy, even on a young tree, and gradually peels in strips. The leaves are unusual and exceptionally attractive, revealing the relationship of *Leucosidea* to the rose. They are compound, with deeply and neatly serrated leaflets. The flowers are quite pretty too, pale greenish-yellow, and borne in sprays. *Leucosidea* is often used as a nest site by small birds.
Propagation: Seed.
Uses: *Leucosidea* can be trimmed into an adequate shade tree, but is best left to grow thick and shrubby. The tree can be grown as a specimen or as a dense screen. On a large scale, it can be used to revegetate degraded streams or to provide shelter for domestic stock. Growth rate is 80 cm per year, if rainfall is high. *Leucosidea* cannot stand a hot summer and only survives drought in cooler areas if planted next to water.

Create communities Place trees that naturally share an unusual habitat together. This copies a natural community, and enables any special treatment, for example in soil preparation, to be concentrated where it is needed.

Loxostylis alata
Tierhout

Size: 3–7 x 4–9 m (wild), up to 4 x 5 m (garden)
Natural habitat: *Loxostylis* occurs in the coastal strip from the southern Cape to KwaZulu-Natal. It is found in scrub and on forest margins, nearly always on rocky outcrops.
Growth form: It is a small, thickset tree, usually branching low down. *Loxostylis* has exceptional foliage. The leaves are a deep glossy green and divided into many small, slender, pointed leaflets. New growth is bright red, with deep red dots scattered on a paler background. Red flushes appear throughout the year, not just in spring. The flowers are small conical stars, produced in exuberant bunches. Sexes are separate on different trees. Male flowers are white. Female flowers are superficially similar, but are surrounded by red sepals, which dominate the tree once the white petals have fallen. They are dry, so remain in good condition for some time.
Propagation: Seed, which must be fresh.
Uses: *Loxostylis* produces a pretty specimen after two years and flowering begins at four years. It could also be used as a screen, and, with pruning, as a small shade tree. Growth rate is about 70 cm per year, given warm summers and high rainfall. It grows surprisingly well in a temperate summer, provided that rainfall is adequate, and can tolerate slight frost.

Macaranga capensis
Wild poplar

Size: 8–15 x 9–17 m (wild), up to 11 x 12 m (garden)
Natural habitat: *Macaranga* is found naturally on the KwaZulu-Natal and Eastern Cape coasts. It occurs in swamp forest, alongside streams and in other damp spots.
Growth form: It is a large tree with a broad canopy. The leaves are very large with neat veining, and are exceptionally handsome. The fruits are small, but are quickly snapped up by birds, especially rameron pigeons. *Macaranga* is important in maintaining watercourses. Its roots form a mat, lining stream beds, and interweave across the stream to create small weirs. Stable ponds build up behind the weirs and stream velocity is reduced, minimising erosion.
Propagation: Seed, but collecting tiny seedlings beneath a parent tree is more practical.
Uses: Although virtually confined to wet habitats in the wild, *Macaranga* grows perfectly well in an ordinary garden, provided that the summer is warm and rainfall high. It makes a good shade tree, and the combination of its large size and exuberant foliage makes *Macaranga* the perfect focal point for a big tropical feature. First fruiting occurs at about five years. It is also ideal for repairing eroded stream banks on a large scale. Growth is extremely fast, at least 1 m per year.

Garden design Scale is important in a garden. Choose small trees for a small garden. Care about what happens in years to come and don't be one of those who say, 'I won't be there to worry about it.'

Markhamia zanzibarica
Bean tree

Size: 3–6 x 2–4 m (wild), up to 4 x 3 m (garden)
Natural habitat: *Markhamia* occurs naturally in the eastern Lowveld where it is found mainly on rocky hillsides.
Growth form: It is a rather spindly, small tree. The leaves are large and compound, with a furry texture. The vivid flowers reveal the close relationship of this species with the sausage tree, *Kigelia*. However, they are smaller than those of *Kigelia* and the colour pattern is reversed, so that they are bright yellow, veined with maroon. This pattern probably serves as a signpost to pollinators, especially as it is boldest on the petals that serve as a landing platform. The fruit is a very long, thin, loosely twisted structure, which only faintly resembles the giant sausages of *Kigelia*.
Propagation: Seed.
Uses: *Markhamia* makes a nice small specimen, given a hot, dry spot. Flowering begins at four years. Fruiting has not so far been seen outside the natural range. In cultivation, *Markhamia* grows fairly slowly, about 50 cm per year. *Markhamia* is unlikely to thrive in a high-rainfall area, and frost tolerance is probably minimal.

Millettia grandis
Umzimbeet

Size: 8–20 x 11–28 m (wild), up to 10 x 14 m (garden)
Natural habitat: *Millettia* is found on the Eastern Cape and KwaZulu-Natal coasts, where it occurs in evergreen forest.
Growth form: It is a spreading tree with a good canopy. The leaves show seasonal colour changes. New leaves are glossy yellow, the colour being almost masked by the purple-brown veins. Mature leaves are a conventional green. Then in early to mid-summer a deciduous period ensues, the leaves turning pale yellow before falling. This phase can be alarming to the uninitiated gardener who expects leaf fall to occur at a more conventional time, later in the year. The flowers are pea-shaped, deep bright pink and can cover the tree. The fruits are hard, velvety, ginger-coloured pods, with green and gold wefts that glint in bright sunshine. They explode with a loud crack during hot, dry weather, scattering the seeds far and wide.
Propagation: Seed.
Uses: *Millettia* begins to spread at three years; first flowering can be expected then. From four years it makes a good shade tree, and can be recommended for large-scale shade plantings, for example in avenues, sports grounds and municipal parks. Growth rate is about 80 cm per year. *Millettia* grows surprisingly well in places cooler and drier than its natural environment.

Watch your walls Be careful not to plant trees too close to walls. Remember that trees grow out in all directions, so leave enough space behind the tree for normal growth. A tree planted too close to a wall will, of necessity, grow away from the wall at an unnatural angle, and never look its best.

Mimusops obovata
Red milkwood

Size: 4–15 x 3–12 m (wild), up to 9 x 8 m (garden)
Natural habitat: This species ranges northwards along the coastline from the Eastern Cape and is also found inland, in the far northeast. It is most common in coastal lowland forest, but occurs in woodland too.
Growth form: The growth form is upright and *Mimusops* has glossy dark green foliage that casts deep shade. The flowers are little white, hanging stars and make a pleasing, if brief, display. The fruits resemble small orange plums and are borne in great profusion, to the delight of fruit bats and birds.
Propagation: Seed.
Uses: *Mimusops* makes a good shade and specimen tree, and is ideal in a bird garden. In cultivation, *Mimusops* is equally at home at the coast or inland. It flowers in the second year, even when still in the pot, but fruiting has not yet been seen outside the natural range; fruiting begins at four years within the natural range. Growth is reasonably fast, about 60 cm per year. *Mimusops* likes a warm summer, with moderate to good rainfall, and withstands an average winter drought. It tolerates occasional slight frost.

Monodora junodii
Green-apple, Orchid tree

Size: 3–6 x 2–5 m (wild), up to 4 x 3 m (garden)
Natural habitat: *Monodora* has a restricted distribution in Zululand and the eastern Lowveld. It occurs in dry woodland and the understorey of sand forest.
Growth form: The growth form is upright and fairly slender, and the canopy is never dense. The leaves are quite large and are an attractive, glossy, pale green. The flowers are outstanding. They appear in spring when the tree is leafless, and have variously been likened to lanterns and orchids. They are large, with yellowish wings, to which is attached a convoluted structure of deep, lurid red, and they have an almost succulent texture. The fruit (reputedly edible) is a large, dull-coloured, lumpy structure, which turns black when mature.
Propagation: Seed.
Uses: *Monodora* is an ideal small flowering and specimen tree. Flowering and fruiting begin at three years, even well outside the natural range and in a cooler climate. Although *Monodora* tolerates some shade it does not flower well there. Speed of growth is modest, about 40 cm per year. *Monodora* survives slight frost.

Encouraging birds Leaf litter provides a perfect environment for ground-feeding birds, such as thrushes and robins. It also acts as mulch. So avoid an overly tidy garden, as it can become rather sterile.

Morus mesozygia
African mulberry

Size: 10–20 x 10–20 m (wild), up to 13 x 13 m (garden)
Natural habitat: *Morus* has a very restricted distribution, being confined to the northeast corner of Zululand. It is a canopy species, and grows in a variety of forest types.
Growth form: It may be large, with a well-shaped crown. The foliage is outstanding. The leaves are very glossy, neatly serrated with long, thin tips, and have an exquisite vein pattern. The veins appear etched, the three main veins radiating from a common base, the lateral one at right angles to them, and the whole resembling a futuristic railway system. *Morus* is almost evergreen, having a brief deciduous period. The fruits resemble small mulberries.
Propagation: *Morus* is not often seen in cultivation, most likely because seed is hard to find. Small wild seedlings will transplant easily.
Uses: So far, in 15 years of watching, neither flowers nor fruits have been seen in the garden. No matter, for *Morus* is a wonderful feature and a good shade tree. Growth rate is moderate, about 50 cm per year. It likes a warm climate with at least moderate rainfall. It has some drought tolerance, but is unlikely to survive frost.

Noltea africana
Soap dogwood

Size: 2–5 x 2–5 m (wild), up to 3 x 3 m (garden)
Natural habitat: This species is found in the southern Cape where it occurs on forest margins and along stream banks.
Growth form: It is a small upright tree whose branches have a tendency to weep, but it may be shrubby. *Noltea* is most noted for its evergreen foliage. The leaves are long, glossy, narrow and very neatly serrated. They contrast beautifully with the rich purple twigs. The flowers are small and white, but when massed, put on a pleasant display.
Propagation: Seed.
Uses: *Noltea* is worth growing for its flowers and foliage, and makes an adequate screen. Despite being localised in the wild, and a bit of a habitat specialist, it has been 'adopted' by the landscaping trade, perhaps for its versatility. It grows well in Johannesburg for example. Growth is fairly fast, about 70 cm per year, and the tree flowers at three years. *Noltea* needs at least moderate rainfall, but survives normal winter drought.

Buy local Buy your trees from a nursery in your area so that they are 'brought up' under the same conditions as in your garden. For example, people on the Highveld should never buy the bulk of their trees from a coastal or lowveld nursery. It is always fun to try the odd experiment, of course.

Nuxia congesta
Brittle wood, Wildevlier

Size: 3–10 x 3–8 m (wild), up to 4 x 4 m (garden)
Natural habitat: This species is found naturally in the Eastern Cape and much of KwaZulu-Natal and the northeast. It occurs patchily in a variety of wooded habitats.
Growth form: N. congesta is stiffly upright, and more or less evergreen. Leaves are characteristically borne in clusters of three. The flowers are small and white but produced in dense showy masses that attract all sorts of insects. The flowering heads are mushroom-shaped, and can be seen from afar. 'Vlier' is Afrikaans for the European elder, and its use here emphasises the obvious similarity of the flowers of the two species.
Propagation: Seed, which must be collected before the fruits split. It is very fine and best sown under glass.
Uses: N. congesta is very adaptable in cultivation, making a nice flowering specimen. Growth is reasonably quick, about 70 cm per year, and flowering begins at about three years. Nuxia grows best where the rainfall is moderate to good and the summer warm. However, it performs well enough in a temperate summer and withstands an average winter drought.

Nuxia floribunda
Bosvlier, Vlier

Size: 4–10 x 4–10 m (wild), up to 7 x 7 m (garden)
Natural habitat: This is a species of the high-rainfall areas of the Eastern Cape, coastal KwaZulu-Natal and the northeast. It is fairly common in evergreen forests and some particularly fine specimens can be seen from the road running through Oribi Gorge.
Growth form: Upright, and more or less evergreen. Height varies considerably with environment. Older trees develop a deeply fissured bark pattern. The leaves characteristically grow in clusters of three. They are glossy and attractive, with purple stalks and veins. The flowers are small and white, but produced in dense, showy, branching, tree-like bunches that attract all sorts of insects.
Propagation: Seed, which must be collected before the fruits split. It is very fine and best sown under glass.
Uses: N. floribunda is planted mainly for its foliage and flowers, but also makes an adequate shade tree. Growth in cultivation is reasonably quick, about 70 cm per year, and flowering begins at about four years. Nuxia grows best where the rainfall is moderate to good and the summer warm. However, it performs well enough in a temperate summer and withstands an average winter drought.

Indigenous? Indigenous means local, occurring naturally in a defined place. So saying a plant is indigenous to 'South Africa' is too broad a description. For example, a yellow-wood is indigenous to South Africa but would never thrive in the Karoo. You need to chose plants that are indigenous to your area, or will grow well in your garden's conditions.

Ochna arborea
Cape plane

Size: 2–10 x 1–5 m (wild), up to 4 x 2 m (garden)
Natural habitat: *Ochna* ranges from the southern Cape to the warmer parts of the east. It is most common in sand forest, but occurs in other forest types and on rocky slopes too.
Growth form: It is a small slender tree, noted for its bark. This is pale brown in a young tree, but peels as the tree ages to reveal shades of yellow, orange and grey. The leaves are finely serrated and glossy, with embossed parallel veins. New spring growth is brilliant purple, turning red and finally green. *Ochna* has beautiful yellow flowers with wavy petals. They appear in profusion in spring, making a lovely contrast with the red leaves. The fruit consists of black berries attached to the swollen red sepals that once framed the flower, distinctly resembling Mickey Mouse's face. Birds eat the fruits.
Propagation: Seed, which must be fresh. Viability is lost about three days after picking. A practical way to obtain a specimen is to uproot a tiny seedling from beneath a fruiting parent.
Uses: *Ochna* is probably the prettiest of all small trees and it is a great pity that it grows so slowly in cultivation. Growth rarely exceeds 25 cm per year, less under marginal conditions. First flowering occurs at about six years and the lovely bark pattern at 15 years. *Ochna* withstands slight frost.

Olea europaea
Wild olive

Size: 3–10 x 3–8 m (wild), up to 6 x 6 m (garden)
Natural habitat: *Olea* is very widespread, being found almost everywhere except the highest Drakensberg peaks and the deserts of the northwest. It occurs along rivers and in many other habitats too.
Growth form: This tree is usually thickset, and in a harsh environment will be shrubby. However, in warm, wetter areas it can be tall and graceful, with a willow-like quality to its drooping branches. *Olea* has beautiful leaves that are dark grey-green above, much paler below. It has small white flowers that spangle the tree in a cheerful display. *Olea* is noted for the abundance of berries it produces, delighting birds.
Propagation: Seed.
Uses: This is a great character. In cultivation *Olea* retains most of its lower branches, so makes an excellent screen if space permits. With pruning it can be turned into a shade-giving specimen, in conditions that favour fast growth. Whatever the climate, *Olea* is ideal for a bird garden and is the perfect perch for epiphytic orchids, its bark having the right chemistry. Growth rate varies greatly; in very dry or cold areas 30 cm per year is likely, rising to about 80 cm per year if the summer is hot and the rainfall good. *Olea* makes a good bonsai.

Placing your trees Place your big trees very carefully. Remember that you will want shade in summer and sun in winter.

Olinia emarginata
Mountain olinia

Size: 9–25 x 7–20 m (wild), up to 10 x 8 m (garden)
Natural habitat: *Olinia* occurs naturally in the wetter uplands of the east. It is common in montane forest, particularly beside streams, and large specimens grow at Giant's Castle.
Growth form: It is an imposing, upright tree, with a long, clean trunk and dense crown. *Olinia* has very beautiful bark, smooth and mottled in subtle shades of grey and yellow. The leaves are tiny, neat and very glossy. They tremble in the slightest breeze causing the whole tree to shimmer in the sunshine. The flowers are small and white, blushing pink in the centre. Fruiting displays are spectacular. Huge bunches of dark pink berries appear in late autumn, concentrated just beneath the canopy. A fruiting tree is always full of birds, and the berries are a favourite food of the bush blackcap.
Propagation: Seed, but germination is quite slow, taking 6–12 months. Seeds taken from baboon droppings germinate better. Cuttings sometimes strike.
Uses: *Olinia* needs many years to achieve its ultimate magnificence, but makes an attractive feature in the interim. First flowering occurs at seven years, the typical bark pattern having developed nicely then. Growth in warm and temperate summer areas with good rainfall is about 50 cm per year.

Oncoba spinosa
Snuffbox tree

Size: 3–8 x 3–8 m (wild), up to 6 x 5 m (garden)
Natural habitat: *Oncoba* is found on the KwaZulu-Natal coastal plain and to the far northeast. It occurs on the fringes of riverine forest and in other damp, well-wooded habitats.
Growth form: It is a small, semi-deciduous spiny tree, usually upright in form. The edges of the leaves are finely serrated and flush pink in spring. The flowers are very attractive, large, with fine, white, frilly petals surrounding a golden mass of stamens. The fruits resemble small apples but have a woody skin. They are green initially, but blush red from the top downwards as they mature, developing rusty yellow spots just before they fall. Finally, they turn a polished black as they collect on the ground. After they have dried out, the seeds rattle inside the hard skin.
Propagation: Seed.
Uses: *Oncoba* makes a fine small specimen in cultivation. It is also spiny enough to make an adequate barrier. Flowering begins at three years, even outside the species' range and under sub-optimal conditions. Fruiting has not been seen outside the natural range. Growth rate is about 60 cm per year. *Oncoba* grows best where the summer is warm and rainfall high. However, it tolerates fairly low rainfall and slight frost.

Riverine forest Riverine forest lines major rivers and contains mainly trees that can survive or withstand being knocked over by floods. Since they subsist mainly on groundwater supplied from a distant catchment, they do not need high rainfall and riverine forest may extend far into dry country.

Ozoroa engleri
White resin tree

Size: 3–7 x 4–8 m (wild), up to 5 x 5 m (garden)
Natural habitat: *O. engleri* is found naturally in Zululand and the eastern Lowveld. It occurs in open woodland.
Growth form: It branches low down, the trunk and main branches contorting in every direction. The tree's leaves have beautifully marked veins and are bluish-green above, silvery below. The flowers are small and white, and produced in masses. They attract small brightly coloured beetles. Fruits grow only on female trees. They are small and glossy, initially green, marked with streaked black, becoming black and wrinkled. They smell strongly of resin when crushed. Hornbills eat them. 
Propagation: Seed, but germination is poor, best results being obtained with seeds just turning black. Seedlings do not transplant easily, so plant seeds directly into pots.
Uses: *O. engleri* makes an interesting form and foliage specimen. Growth is fairly quick, about 60 cm per year, and first flowering takes place at five years. Fruiting was first noted outside the natural range at 13 years. *O. engleri* likes a warm summer with moderate rainfall.

Ozoroa obovata
Broad-leaved resin tree

Size: 3–6 x 4–7 m (wild), up to 5 x 5 m (garden)
Natural habitat: *O. obovata* is restricted to the Zululand coastal plain. It occurs sparingly in dune forest and in forest patches in the sandy areas around St Lucia.
Growth form: The growth form is fairly stiff and upright, but the tree branches quite low down. The leaves have beautifully marked veins and are bluish-green above, silvery below. The flowers are small and white, and produced in masses in late summer. They attract all manner of insects, especially small brightly coloured beetles. The fruits appear in mid-winter, only on female trees. They are small and glossy, initially green, marked with black streaks, becoming black and wrinkled when mature. They smell strongly of resin when crushed. Tinker barbets and the sombre bulbul eat them.
Propagation: Seed, but germination is poor, best results being obtained with seeds just turning black. Seedlings do not transplant easily, so plant seeds directly into the pots.
Uses: *O. obovata* makes an interesting form and foliage specimen. It is dense enough to make a screen. Growth rate is about 60 cm per year and first flowering takes place at five years. *O. obovata* likes a warm summer with moderate to good rainfall.

Baboon surprise Here's an experiment that is both fun and rewarding. Collect baboon droppings and grow them! You will find out what the baboons have eaten and may well end up with a species of tree that no-one else has grown. Some seeds have to pass through an animal's gut before germinating.

Pancovia golungensis
False soap-berry

Size: 3–6 x 2–5 m (wild), up to 4 x 3 m (garden)
Natural habitat: *Pancovia* is found in Zululand where it occurs in a variety of evergreen forest types. It is quite common in the forest in the Hluhluwe section of the Hluhluwe-Umfolozi Park, and can be seen on the forest walk in the main camp.
Growth form: It is a slender, upright tree. The leaves are large and divided into many leaflets, and the new growth is particularly showy. It is produced in thin pyramids, the new leaves being virtually white, with brilliant red veins. They turn green and fill out later. The fleshy, orange fruits are also striking, and grow in profusion up the main trunk of female trees. Fruit bats like them.
Propagation: Seed.
Uses: *Pancovia* is a good tree for a small garden, being especially useful because it thrives and fruits in partial shade. Fruiting begins at five years, even outside the natural range. Growth rate is modest, about 40 cm per year. *Pancovia* likes a warm climate with good rainfall and is probably sensitive to drought and frost.

Pappea capensis
Doppruim

Size: 4–9 x 5–11 m (wild), up to 6 x 7 m (garden)
Natural habitat: *Pappea* has an unusual distribution that spans not only the typical warm summer-rainfall area of the east but much of the Karoo and Northern Cape as well. It occurs in deciduous woodland.
Growth form: It is a chunky tree with a dense spreading canopy. *Pappea*'s deciduous period is short. The leaves are distinctive, heavily veined and usually neatly serrated. The flowers are insignificant, but the fruits are spectacular. These are green capsules borne only on female trees, which split when mature, revealing a translucent red jelly – irresistible to birds and people alike. Good fruiting displays do not occur every year. A year of plenty is almost always followed by one or more (pessimists say seven) poor or blank years.
Propagation: Seed. *Pappea* dislikes life in a packet and only picks up speed a couple of years after being planted out.
Uses: *Pappea* is a bit of a test of patience, for the sexes are separate and cannot be identified when small. Bird enthusiasts must be prepared to plant at least two trees and to wait eight or more years for the first fruit crop. In the meantime *Pappea* makes a pleasant feature and shade tree. It likes a warm summer and moderate rainfall.

Dealing with frost Remember, frost rolls downhill, so plants at the bottom of a slope or against a wall, where frost can get caught, will be worst affected. Be selective in early plantings, for tender trees will be sheltered by well-grown tougher species planted first. There is rarely frost near a house's north-facing wall, as it tends to retain heat overnight.

Pavetta edentula
Large-leaved bride's bush

Size: 3–8 x 2–6 m (wild), up to 4 x 3 m (garden)
Natural habitat: This species is found naturally in Zululand and eastern Mpumalanga. It occurs on north-facing, grassy hills, usually among rocks.
Growth form: *Pavetta* is a small, thickset tree. At maturity the bark is a pale smoky brown, with the texture of stiff velvet, finely fissured in a spiral pattern. The leaves bear bacterial nodules, which appear as regularly spaced black streaks. These represent an interesting example of symbiosis: the bacterium enjoying a secure home while fixing atmospheric nitrogen into a form the plant can use. The flowers are white, vivid yet delicate, sweetly scented and produced in such masses as to cover the plant. The fruit is a small black berry greatly liked by birds. 
Propagation: Seed or cuttings.
Uses: *Pavetta* can be grown as a pride-of-place specimen or as part of a shrubbery and is suitable for a bird garden, even when space is limited. First flowering occurs at about four years. Initial growth rate is about 30 cm per year. It likes a warm spot, with moderate rainfall, and tolerates slight frost.

Peddiea africana
Green flower tree

Size: 2–4 x 2–3 m (wild), up to 4 x 3 m (garden)
Natural habitat: This species is common in the warm, evergreen forests of the east. It is usually found in the dense shade of the forest interior, sometimes in partial shade at the forest edge.
Growth form: It is small and slender, with dark, shiny, sword-shaped leaves. The flowers are unusual and most attractive, consisting of clusters of thin, trumpet-like tubes. The flowers are pale green, but may be variably tinged with red, especially on trees growing inland. They give off a sweet scent at night. The fruits are black and glossy, and resemble miniature plums. They are reputedly toxic to humans. Fruiting peaks in mid-winter.
Propagation: Seed.
Uses: *Peddiea* is one of the finest of all small trees in cultivation. Although confined to shady places in the wild, it grows much better in full sun in the garden. Growth rate is nearly 1 m per year. Flowering begins at three years, and at five years continues almost throughout the year. *Peddiea* can be used as a dainty specimen in a tiny garden or as a contrast feature in a flowerbed. It likes a temperate to warm climate with at least moderate rainfall.

Weedeating dangers Beware of weedeaters as they can do fatal damage to trees, especially young trees. The flailing nylon string soon cuts the bark all the way round and the tree is cut off from its food and water supply. The tree is in effect 'ring-barked'.

Peltophorum africanum
Weeping wattle, Huilboom

Size: 4–9 x 5–11 m (wild), up to 8 x 10 m (garden)
Natural habitat: *Peltophorum* is found in Zululand and most of the northeast. It is locally common in deciduous woodland.
Growth form: It is upright in form while young, spreading later and casting a good shade. It superficially resembles an acacia, the leaves being compound, divided into countless tiny leaflets, which give the foliage a feathery look. Growing points are covered with rust-coloured hairs, and expanding new leaves unfurl in the style of a fern. *Peltophorum* can be briefly deciduous. The flowers are bright yellow, with fine, crinkly petals, and put on a brilliant show in early summer. The fruits are flat pods, which hang in bunches for a long period.
Propagation: Seed.
Uses: *Peltophorum* makes a good garden tree. Growth is fast, about 1 m per year. A respectable shade tree results after four years, making it a good tree to use in avenues. Flowering may begin at two years and is reliably profuse after five years. *Peltophorum* thrives in a wide range of climates but does not enjoy a cool, wet summer.

Phoenix reclinata
Wild date palm

Size: 3–9 x 3–7 m (wild), up to 5 x 5 m (garden)
Natural habitat: *Phoenix* is found naturally on the coastal plain and adjacent low-lying valleys, from Port Elizabeth northwards, and also occurs in the eastern Lowveld. It nearly always lines riverbanks, leaning over the water with tropical languor.
Growth form: *Phoenix* can be single-stemmed and upright, but is usually multi-stemmed, with at least some of the trunks reclining. The tree's leaves are huge, 3–4 m long, divided into many narrow leaflets, and very spiny at the base. They arc gracefully. The fruits make a fine display on female trees. They are orange, thinly fleshy and produced in bunches of hundreds. Bulbuls and barbets are especially fond of them. *Phoenix* is host to the butterfly *Zophopetes dysmephila*.
Propagation: Seed.
Uses: *Phoenix* makes a fine accent plant next to water, whether as a solo specimen or mixed with low-growing, large-leafed plants. It is also worth including in a suitable bird garden. Growth rate next to water, in a warm environment, is over 1 m per year; much less in poorer conditions. Age of first fruiting is about five years. On a larger scale, *Phoenix* can be used to stabilise the banks of degraded rivers, because it has a spreading root system that holds down soil.

Year-round birds To attract birds to your garden throughout the year, try planting a number of different fruiting trees, rather than focusing on just one prolific species. Fill your garden with a variety of trees, which fruit at different times of year.

Pittosporum viridiflorum
Kasuur

Size: 3–10 x 3–8 m (wild), up to 6 x 5 m (garden)
Natural habitat: *Pittosporum* is locally common over much of the south and east of the country. It occurs in almost every habitat, especially in small forest clumps and on rocky outcrops. It is equally at home at sea level and high in the mountains.
Growth form: *Pittosporum* is a dense tree with a chunky crown. The leaves are very dark and glossy when first expanded. The flowers are pale yellow, sweet scented and grow in dense bunches. This tree's fruiting displays are most attractive. The fruits are a dull pale brown initially, but when mature they split to reveal bright orange seeds, which are coated with a glistening jelly. Birds are very partial to them.
Propagation: Seed.
Uses: This is an attractive tree that can either be used for screening in its early career or shaped into a small shade tree. It is also an asset in a wildlife garden. Speed of growth is moderate, about 40 cm per year. First fruiting occurs at about four years. *Pittosporum* is a very useful species in the garden, as it tolerates a wide range of different environments, but it grows best where rainfall is moderate to good.

Podocarpus falcatus
Outeniqua yellowwood

Size: 10–45 x 8–35 m (wild), up to 20 x 17 m (garden)
Natural habitat: *P. falcatus* is found in the southern Cape, over most of KwaZulu-Natal and on the eastern Escarpment wherever there are evergreen forests.
Growth form: It is large and majestic. The bark has a regular flaking pattern and is a haven for lichens. The canopy is so dense *P. falcatus* is often used as a roost and nest site by small birds. The berries are yellow and persist on the tree for many months. Parrots, louries, and fruit bats are fond of the fruits. 
Propagation: Seed.
Uses: The wild growth form – a straight trunk capped with a spreading crown – is rarely seen in cultivation, where a pyramidal shape is usual. So, *P. falcatus* is not a good shade tree. Nevertheless, the dense foliage does give the tree a definite presence, making it an attractive feature. In a large garden it can be used as a screen. Its rate of growth is 80 cm per year in deep soil, much less otherwise. Although not common at the coast, *P. falcatus* will grow extremely well in coastal gardens. This tree must be grown in garden that gets moderate to good rainfall.

Getting rid of pests without chemicals The rules of chemical use in the garden are simple – DON'T. Pick larger pests off your trees by hand, or spray soapy water over infestations of tiny pests. Rarely is either necessary on indigenous plants, which co-exist happily with local invertebrates.

Podocarpus henkelii
Henkel's yellowwood

Size: 10–20 x 10–20 m (wild), up to 12 x 12 m (garden)
Natural habitat: *P. henkelii* is a localised endemic, being found only in mist-belt forest in the west of KwaZulu-Natal and in the Eastern Cape.
Growth form: It is a spreading tree, with a heavy canopy and comparatively short trunk. The bark is neatly and deeply fissured in a spiral pattern. The leaves are long and pointed, and both they and the branches droop gracefully, creating a Christmas-tree effect. There are no flowers in the conventional sense, as yellowwoods are conifers, although they bear little resemblance to their relatives, the pines. The female 'cones' are fleshy and look like large green berries, even when ripe.
Propagation: Seed.
Uses: In cultivation it is the most rewarding of the yellowwoods. The tree's shape will be pyramidal, many branches being retained near ground level. So, this is not a shade tree, but in a large garden can be used as a screen. The spiral bark pattern appears at about five years. Note that only female trees bear cones, and then only when at least 10 years old. The speed of growth is fairly slow, 30–40 cm per year being likely. *P. henkelii* likes high rainfall. In dry areas it is less successful, especially where the summers are hot.

Podocarpus latifolius
Real yellowwood

Size: 8–30 x 7–25 m (wild), up to 12 x 10 m (garden)
Natural habitat: This species has much the same distribution as *P. falcatus*. It is most common in the mist-belt forests and also occurs in montane forests.
Growth form: *P. latifolius* is a large, dark, upright tree. On older specimens the bark develops characteristic long, flaky, vertical strips. The leaves are distinctly bluish, and the foliage can look almost black at a distance. Bursts of new growth are pale mauve, fading to almost white before assuming their mature colour. The berries are grey, but are seated upon a purple, plum-like receptacle and can be showy. They are popular with fruit bats as well as birds.
Propagation: Seed.
Uses: Planting a yellowwood such as *P. latifolius* is to create a living museum. Yellowwoods are deeply ingrained in South Africa's heritage and recent history. They are also remnants of an earlier age, most of their kin banished to the colder regions of the earth by the advent of the more vigorous flowering plants. *P. latifolius* tends to retain its lower branches in cultivation. These can be pruned, but the tree always looks as though it has had a bad haircut. It grows about 40 cm per year. It grows best in high rainfall.

Getting the ideal form When selecting a tree for its form, it is important to remember that the 'ideal' form is often only adopted if the tree is grown in the open, away from all competition. However, a few forest trees require just the opposite and must be given some shade during their formative years – *Podocarpus* is a good example.

Protea roupelliae
Silver protea

Size: 3–6 x 2–5 m (wild), up to 4 x 3 m (garden)
Natural habitat: *P. roupelliae* occurs in the summer-rainfall, eastern grasslands, ranging from the south coast of KwaZulu-Natal through the uplands to the eastern Escarpment.
Growth form: It is rugged in shape. The leaves have a silvery tinge and glint in sun and wind. They always look immaculate because they are never browsed (the nitrogen content is so low that it will not support animal life). The flowering head varies in colour from pale pink to red. *P. roupelliae* is a great producer of nectar and is the favourite food plant of the malachite sunbird and Gurney's sugarbird. The latter nests almost exclusively in this tree.
Propagation: Seed, which must be collected from dried flower heads, and is ready once new shoots have grown up past the heads. Germination is improved by first soaking the seeds for 30 minutes in water at 50 °C, air-drying the seeds afterwards. Dust fungicide onto the seeds before planting.
Uses: *P. roupelliae* makes a good flowering and foliage specimen, and is an asset in a bird garden. Growth rate is moderate, about 50 cm per year, and flowering begins at four years. It grows best on a slope with good drainage, in a temperate climate with moderate to high rainfall.

Protorhus longifolia
Red beech

Size: 6–15 x 5–13 m (wild), up to 11 x 9 m (garden)
Natural habitat: *Protorhus* is found naturally in the Eastern Cape, the KwaZulu-Natal coast and the eastern Escarpment. It occurs in warm forests and on cliff edges.
Growth form: It is an erect evergreen tree with a rounded crown and dense foliage. The leaves are pretty, long and narrow, and neatly veined. At all times of year a few will be preparing for 'autumn' by turning yellow or red. Spring flushes are also red. The flowers are modest, tiny, brick-red stars, and fruit is produced in abundance in mid-summer. Mature berries are a pale lilac-grey, and eaten by birds. Most trees seem to fruit, but there are a few trees that have only male flowers, so cannot fruit.
Propagation: Seed.
Uses: *Protorhus* can be greatly recommended for the garden. It is a must for foliage and tends to keep its lower branches, so makes a better screen than a shade tree. It also makes a regularly shaped specimen, and could be used as a component of a bird garden. Growth rate is about 80 cm per year. It grows best in warm areas with good rainfall, but tolerates a little frost.

Shimmering leaves A leaf will have a silvery or grey tinge if all its hairs are aligned and flattened in the same direction. Leaf hairs reduce wind speed over the leaf surface and so help to reduce evaporation. The flattened hair layer reflects light and can shimmer when it is windy and the sun is shining.

Prunus africana
Bitter almond, Red stinkwood

Size: 10–25 x 10–22 m (wild), up to 12 x 12 m (garden)
Natural habitat: *Prunus* occurs naturally in the Eastern Cape, the temperate parts of KwaZulu-Natal and the eastern Escarpment. It is confined to evergreen forest and is locally common in the mist-belt.
Growth form: *Prunus* is a tall, imposing tree, with a spreading crown when mature. The trunk is straight, with grey bark cracking in a characteristic oblong pattern. The leaves are dark and glossy, and cast dense shade throughout the year. When crushed they have a lovely almond scent. The fruits are fleshy and deep purple, and very popular with birds, especially the rameron pigeon and Knysna lourie.
Propagation: Seed. Birds usually eat the whole lot, so often the only option is to uproot seedlings that birds plant along forest paths or in farm gardens within the tree's natural range.
Uses: *Prunus* makes a wonderful feature or shade tree and is perfect for a bird garden. Fruiting begins at about seven years. Growth is rapid, up to 1 m per year if rainfall is good and the climate temperate. *Prunus* thrives in a cool climate, provided that the frost is not too severe. It does not enjoy heat and survives only an average winter drought.

Ptaeroxylon obliquum
Sneezewood

Size: 4–22 x 3–18 m (wild), up to 16 x 12 m (garden)
Natural habitat: *Ptaeroxylon* is found throughout most of the southeast and east of the country. It is locally common in mist-belt forest, less so in coastal forest. It also occurs on cliff edges and in deciduous woodland.
Growth form: Growth form depends upon environment. Forest specimens are tall and straight, open-grown trees are short and branch low down. The bark of older trees is furrowed in a beautiful pattern. The leaves have a pleasant smell when crushed. The flowers are yellow and produced in showy bunches in spring, when the tree is nearly leafless. The fruits are capsules, which split to release winged seeds.
Propagation: Seed, which must be collected just before the fruits split. Alternatively, wrap unripe fruits in a stocking while still attached to the tree and collect the seeds at leisure.
Uses: *Ptaeroxylon* is well worth growing for its form, foliage and flowers, and would make a good avenue tree. A nice little shade tree results after four years. First flowering occurs at about six years. Growth is fairly fast, nearly 1 m per year if the rainfall is good and summer warm. *Ptaeroxylon* might prove a commercial timber proposition. It has the finest wood of any indigenous tree and grows better than any rival species.

Sneezewood The wood of *Ptaeroxylon obliquum*, sneezewood, is incredibly tough and long-lasting. Early farmers used it to make fence posts – many of them still standing, untouched by termites or rot, due to the wood's unique chemicals. The sawdust induces nasal irritation, hence the common name.

Pteleopsis myrtifolia
Myrtle bushwillow

Size: 4–8 x 3–7 m (wild), up to 6 x 5 m (garden)
Natural habitat: *Pteleopsis* occurs naturally in the Lowveld and northern Zululand, and is most common in sandy soil. It may dominate sand forest.
Growth form: *Pteleopsis* is slender when young, most of its branches held upright. Only in later life, and if space permits, does it spread. The bark is smooth and very pale grey, gradually accumulating a cover of lichens. The leaves are glossy, delicate, and never cast full shade. The small white flowers make a massed display in late summer. The fruits have two or three papery wings. At first greenish-yellow, they mature to pale brown, and drape the tree for several months. 
Propagation: Seed, although the germination rate, even of apparently sound seed, is low. Wild seed is heavily parasitised.
Uses: *Pteleopsis* is delightful at all ages. Fruiting takes place outside the natural range and first occurs at about six years. Growth rate is about 50 cm per year, provided that the summer is warm and rainfall moderate. *Pteleopsis* can cope with high rainfall provided that drainage is good.

Pterocarpus rotundifolius
Round-leaf kiaat

Size: 3–9 x 2–7 m (wild), up to 7 x 5 m (garden)
Natural habitat: This is a species of the eastern Lowveld. It is a sparse component of deciduous woodland or may form single-species stands in otherwise treeless grassland.
Growth form: Kruger National Park specimens tend to be stunted and multi-stemmed, the result of browsing by animals and fire. When these factors are removed, a slender, upright tree with a graceful branching pattern results. *Pterocarpus* has exceptionally beautiful foliage. The leaves are compound, and they are divided into regularly spaced, round and glossy leaflets. There is a very short deciduous period. The flowers are a bright yellow and borne in profusion in mid-summer. The fruit is a thin, flat pod.
Propagation: Seed or cuttings.
Uses: *Pterocarpus* makes a wonderful garden specimen. The age of first flowering varies considerably. Newly struck cuttings may flower in their first year, yet a well-grown six-year-old has failed to flower. Growth is quick, about 1 m per year, given a warm summer with moderate rainfall and a frost-free winter. *Pterocarpus* has great potential in dried arrangements, as the cut foliage dries to a rich copper colour (rather like copper beech) and does not disintegrate for at least two years.

Frost prevention myth There is a famous myth that it is possible to protect a frosted tree by hosing it with water before sunrise. This cannot possibly work because the frost damage has already been done, even if it does not yet show.

Pterocelastrus tricuspidatus
Cherrywood, Kershout

Size: 4–9 x 4–9 m (wild), up to 6 x 6 m (garden)
Natural habitat: *Pterocelastrus* ranges from the southwestern Cape, through KwaZulu-Natal, to the eastern Escarpment. It is found in evergreen forest, denser woodland and on rock outcrops. Large, elegant specimens can be seen near Port Elizabeth.
Growth form: This tree is sturdy in form. The leaves are dark, rounded and glossy, and leathery in texture. The flowers are white and small, but are sweetly scented and grow in masses. They are followed by delightful fruits, little orange lanterns resembling Christmas tree decorations.
Propagation: Seed.
Uses: In cultivation *Pterocelastrus* is a worker, as well as a modest beauty. If open-grown, it retains most of its lower branches and makes a good screen. With a little pruning it makes a passable shade tree. This tree enjoys a cool or temperate climate and moderate to good rainfall. However, its tolerance of drought and fairly severe frost makes it especially useful in marginal areas where little else will grow.

Rapanea melanophloeos
Cape beech

Size: 3–11 x 3–9 m (wild), up to 7 x 7 m (garden)
Natural habitat: *Rapanea* occurs naturally in the wetter parts of South Africa, ranging from the southwestern Cape to the eastern Escarpment. It is common in evergreen forests, from lowland swamps to the highest mountain kloofs.
Growth form: It is a solidly built tree, with lovely foliage. The leaves are thick, almost succulent, and deep rich green. This contrasts beautifully with the purple leaf stalks and young shoots. The flowers are tiny, but borne in interesting star-shaped bunches along bare twigs, behind the leaves. Large crops of dark purple berries follow, to the delight of birds.
Propagation: Seed.
Uses: *Rapanea* makes a very pretty specimen after four years, and it never gets too big. Fruiting has been noted at three years and is prolific after about six, making this tree essential in a suitable bird garden. Rate of growth is moderate, about 50 cm per year. *Rapanea* grows best where rainfall is good and the summer temperate to warm. Moderate rainfall suffices if the summer is not too hot. This tree survives slight frost. However, it withstands considerable cold if planted on the north face of an existing shrubbery or bush clump.

Flowers Flowers have been part of human culture at least since Neanderthal people placed them in the graves of their dead. Flowering trees were planted in the Egypt of the Pharaohs. The botanist Linnaeus forthrightly described flowers as 'sex organs, usually blatantly displayed'.

Raphia australis
Kosi palm

Size: 12–20 x 10–16 m (wild), up to 14 x 12 m (garden)
Natural habitat: In South Africa, it occurs naturally only in Kosi Bay. The population at Mtunzini is descended from commercial planting in 1915. *Raphia* is confined to swamp forest.
Growth form: It is a large palm, with a 10-m trunk. The leaves are up to 18 m long, reputedly the world's largest. They curve out and eventually down. The flowers form a large, branching, off-white mass. The fruits grow in large bunches, resembling highly polished, tightly closed pine cones. They are the favourite food of the palmnut vulture, a tropical bird that nests only in *Raphia* and extends into South Africa wherever this tree is established. 
Propagation: Seed. Germination may take six months.
Uses: An established young tree grows quickly, 1 m or more per year. A warm summer is essential, but swampy conditions are not – high rainfall will do just as well. Nevertheless, *Raphia* looks its best planted next to water, and its outstanding specimen qualities are enhanced if trees are planted 3–6 m apart, forming a grove. *Raphia* dies when about 30 years old, and falls over soon afterwards, so must be sited appropriately.

Rauvolfia caffra
Quinine tree

Size: 7–20 x 6–18 m (wild), up to 12 x 10 m (garden)
Natural habitat: *Rauvolfia* is found along the southeastern coast and the immediate interior, extending into the far northeast. It occurs in evergreen forest, either alongside streams or in swamps.
Growth form: It is tall and elegant. The bark is smooth and pale on a young tree, later darkening and developing furrows. The dark, glossy leaves are exquisite, very long and narrow. *Rauvolfia* is almost evergreen, new pale green growth appearing before the last of the old leaves are shed. The flowers are small and white, but borne in bunches and make a nice display. The fruits resemble large berries, and are black when ripe. A heavy crop is produced about every other year and is extremely popular with birds and fruit bats.
Propagation: Seed, often planted in gardens by birds.
Uses: *Rauvolfia* is a brilliant garden subject. It makes an ideal shade tree or background foliage in a large garden. First flowering occurs at five years. Fruiting takes place outside the natural range: it is prolific in Cape Town. *Rauvolfia* is a must in a suitable bird garden. Growth is rapid, about 1.2 m per year. *Rauvolfia* enjoys high rainfall or a high water table, and will thrive in a soggy spot unsuitable for much else.

Watering If you have planted your tree properly (see Introduction), you should not have to water it ever again. The water that drained away in the initial preparation is still down there and is sucked up as the ground dries out. This should last until the next natural rain.

Rhamnus prinoides
Dogwood

Size: 3–5 x 4–7 m (wild), up to 4 x 6 m (garden)
Natural habitat: *Rhamnus* ranges from the far north of the eastern Escarpment, through the KwaZulu-Natal Midlands and Free State, to the southern Cape. It can be very common on forest margins, alongside streams and in grassland, provided that rocks are present to shelter it from fire.
Growth form: *Rhamnus* is often shrubby and tends to form a rounded bush. The foliage is very dark and glossy, and *Rhamnus* is evergreen throughout the winter drought, no matter how severe the frost. The flowers are small white stars, which contrast with the near-blackness of the leaves. The fruits are small berries, at first pale green, changing to red and then black. Small birds are very fond of them.
Propagation: Seed.
Uses: *Rhamnus* is exceptionally useful. Its extreme frost-hardiness means that it can be used as a specimen, evergreen screen, or component of a bird garden, in the very coldest parts of the country. It also thrives in warm areas, provided that rainfall is high. The only climate that it cannot handle is a hot and dry one. Rate of growth is 1 m per year in a damp climate, much less otherwise. The cut foliage makes an excellent and long-lasting addition to flower arrangements.

Rhus chirindensis
Redcurrant, Bostaaibos

Size: 4–15 x 3–13 m (wild), up to 9 x 7 m (garden)
Natural habitat: It occurs in the coastal belt from the south-western Cape, to Zululand, the KwaZulu-Natal Midlands, and up the eastern Escarpment. It is common in coastal and mist-belt forests, woodlands, and scrub in hot valleys.
Growth form: It can be a tall, straight tree, or shrubby if it has been browsed. The leaves are large and elegant, casting complete shade for much of the year. The bark is smooth, except for the occasional large spine. The flowers are very small, but produced in profusion, and attract many tiny insects. Little berries follow, produced in cascades that attract small fruit-eating birds, notably white-eyes. Flowering and fruiting usually begin at two years. Only female trees bear fruit.
Propagation: Seed or cuttings.
Uses: It makes a shade tree in four years and a good central feature in a bird garden or bush clump. It is somewhat prone to attack by pests. One garden specimen endured a fungal attack on its growing tips, ring-barking of all young shoots by an unknown agency, and total defoliation at the jaws of a hawkmoth caterpillar. *R. chirindensis*' response is to branch and grow new sets of leaves, whatever the time of year. Growth is rapid, over 1 m per year in a warm, damp climate.

Muddled monikers The common names of trees are sometimes fun and very descriptive, but they can also be duplicated and muddling. Think of blinkblaar (shiny leaf), a name sometimes given to both *Rhamnus prinoides* and *Ziziphus mucronata*, totally unrelated species. Their scientific names are unique.

Rhus lancea
Karee

Size: 4–10 x 5–12 m (wild), up to 8 x 9 m (garden)
Natural habitat: *R. lancea* is the most widespread and best-known *Rhus*, being common in every province except KwaZulu-Natal. It grows in a variety of habitats, especially in dry woodland, on koppies and alongside streams.
Growth form: It can be single-stemmed and spreading, or shrubby. Leaves are divided into three long, narrow, elegant leaflets. Masses of tiny white flowers appear in mid- to late winter. The sweet scent and buzz of bees that are attracted to the flowers are obvious from some distance. The fruits are also tiny, thin-fleshed berries, which attract small fruit-eating birds, and grow in cascades. Flowering and fruiting begin in the third year. Only female trees bear fruit.
Propagation: Seed or cuttings.
Uses: *R. lancea* is a good shade tree and attracts birds. It makes a good tall screen, suitable for very large gardens or farms, and is ideal for planting alongside dams where frost collects. *R. lancea* survives the most severe frosts and long droughts, and is almost impossible to kill. So, it is essential in landscaping work where subsequent neglect is likely. Even in very cold, dry areas a growth rate of 60 cm per year can be expected, doubling if the climate is warmer and wetter.

Rhus leptodictya
Mountain karee

Size: 3–8 x 3–8 m (wild), up to 6 x 5 m (garden)
Natural habitat: This species is widespread in the Free State, and further north and east. It is found in a variety of wooded habitats, particularly on koppies and rocky hillsides.
Growth form: It is upright in form and may be shrubby. The branches have a tendency to weep. The leaves are large and neatly serrated along the edges. *R. leptodictya* is almost evergreen, thinning a little during winter if drought or cold is prolonged. The flowers are tiny, but produced in profusion, attracting many insects, and insect-eating birds such as warblers and shrikes. They are followed by tiny, thin-fleshed berries, produced in cascades, which attract small fruit-eating birds. Flowering and fruiting usually begin in the third year. Only female trees produce fruit.
Propagation: Seed or cuttings.
Uses: *R. leptodictya* makes a beautiful specimen in cultivation. It looks good in a large north-facing rockery. It grows large enough to make a modest shade tree and the foliage is exceptionally graceful. It is ideal in a bird garden. The growth rate is reasonably fast, about 70 cm per year.

Shade trees for cold and warm gardens In cold areas, plant *Celtis africana* (as it is deciduous and will let sun through in winter), *Rhus lancea* or *Acacia karroo*; in warm areas, you can plant *Trichilia*, as it gives dense shade, or use *Albizia* for a dappled effect.

Rhus pallens
Warty taaibos

Size: 3–6 x 3–6 m (wild), up to 5 x 5 m (garden)
Natural habitat: This species is widespread in warm, drier areas, extending along the coastal belt from the southwestern Cape to Zululand, and throughout much of the eastern interior. It is locally common in woodland.
Growth form: *R. pallens* grows into a chunky tree. The leaves have a winged stalk and are shiny, gleaming when young as though varnished. The foliage is dense and evergreen. The bark bears small warts arranged in a regular and distinctive fashion. The flowers are tiny, but produced in profusion, and for a short period attract many insects and insectivorous birds. The fruits are also tiny, red-brown and thin-fleshed berries, produced in cascades that attract small fruit-eating birds, notably white-eyes. Flowering and fruiting usually begin at two years. Only female trees bear fruit.
Propagation: Seed or cuttings.
Uses: *R. pallens* makes a nice specimen, component of a bush clump or a perfect wild hedge, and is essential in a bird garden. Ideally it should be planted in threes or greater numbers, both for effect and to improve chances of including both sexes, and hence fruiting. It grows quickly, 1 m or so per year. It grows best where the summer is warm.

Rhus pyroides
Fire thorn, Common taaibos

Size: 3–7 x 3–8 m (wild), up to 5 x 6 m (garden)
Natural habitat: This species occurs almost everywhere in South Africa, except the winter-rainfall and arid areas. The tree is fairly common in dry woodland and among rocks in grassland. Lovely specimens can be seen on Melville Koppies.
Growth form: Occasionally shrubby, it often makes a nicely shaped weeping tree. The leaves are larger than those of most other *Rhus*. In a cold, dry autumn they may turn a rich yellow, prior to a brief deciduous period. The young trunk and branches often have large spines. The flowers are tiny, but produced in profusion, and for a short period attract many insects and insectivorous birds. The fruits are small, yellowish berries, produced in cascades that attract small fruit-eating birds. Flowering and fruiting usually begin in the third year. Only female trees produce fruit.
Propagation: Seed or cuttings.
Uses: *R. pyroides* makes a small shade tree or specimen, or a good component of a bush clump, especially in a bird garden. Ideally plant three or more. This improves the chance of including a female, and outside the natural range a male must be present too, if the female is to be pollinated. It grows about 70 cm per year.

Local and exotic The trifoliolate leaf of *Rhus* distinguishes indigenous species from an exotic, often called *Rhus*, but more appropriately, *Toxicodendron succedanea*, which is widely cultivated. The latter has pinnate leaves and causes allergies in sensitive people. Indigenous *Rhus* are harmless.

Rinorea angustifolia
White violet-bush

Size: 2–6 x 2–4 m (wild), up to 4 x 3 m (garden)
Natural habitat: *Rinorea* occurs naturally in most of KwaZulu-Natal and the eastern Escarpment. It is common in mist-belt forest, much less so in coastal forest, and is found almost invariably in deep shade.
Growth form: It is erect in habit, even if shrubby. The leaves are small and dainty, deep rich green, with a dazzling gloss, and the leaf edges are finely toothed. The flowers are no less attractive, small thin white trumpets borne in profusion towards the branch tips. They have a sweet smell. The fruits are explosive capsules. The very rare spotted thrush nests almost exclusively in *Rinorea*.
Propagation: Seed. Fruits must be picked just before full maturity and stored in a cloth bag if seed is to be collected.
Uses: *Rinorea* makes the perfect garden plant, and must be put in a prominent place where all visitors can admire it. Despite living in the shade in the wild it grows much better in full sunshine. Flowering begins at two years. Growth rate is about 40 cm per year. *Rinorea* likes moderate to high rainfall and a temperate to warm summer. Frost tolerance is slight, but its small size enables you to protect it by tucking it into frost-free corners of your garden.

Rothmannia capensis
Candlewood

Size: 4–8 x 3–7 m (wild), up to 5 x 4 m (garden)
Natural habitat: *R. capensis* is a fairly widespread species, extending from the southern Cape to KwaZulu-Natal and much of the northeast. It is particularly common along cliff edges in warm areas.
Growth form: It is a sturdy tree with a good canopy. The leaves are glossy, and have little pits on the under-surface, reputedly inhabited by unique mites, but these are minute, and invisible to the naked eye. The bark develops a neat, square, cracked pattern with age. The flowers are bell-shaped, sweetly scented and quite large, and make beautiful displays by any standards. They are very pale yellow, variably streaked with maroon, and appear in mid-summer. Large spherical fruits follow, which are green even when mature. Monkeys eat them once they soften.
Propagation: Seed, which must be fresh.
Uses: *R. capensis* makes the perfect flowering specimen: it does not get too large and the foliage is attractive year round. First flowering usually occurs at three years. It can also be used as a small shade tree or a screen. Rate of growth is moderate, about 50 cm per year. *R. capensis* likes moderate to high rainfall but withstands moderate drought and some frost.

Planting in clay Clay soil is not good for using in seed trays or pots, as it tends to cake solid. If this is all you have, mix liberally with sand and well-rotted compost.

Rothmannia globosa
September bells

Size: 3–8 x 2–6 m (wild), up to 5 x 4 m (garden)
Natural habitat: *R. globosa* is common in the warm, wetter parts of the east. It is confined to evergreen forest, either in the understorey or on the margins.
Growth form: The growth habit is slender and upright. Older specimens develop an interesting bark pattern, a perfectly square cross-hatching, like embossed hessian. The leaves have bright red central veins. The flowers are bell-shaped, sweetly scented and quite large, and make beautiful displays by any standards. They are white, with pale pink throats, and appear almost without fail in September.
Propagation: Seed, which must be fresh.
Uses: *R. globosa* makes an excellent flowering specimen. In cultivation this tree grows best in full sun, and often flowers more prolifically than wild specimens. It also grows reasonably well in partial shade, but only flowers on the branches that protrude into the open. Usually, first flowering occurs at three years. The tree's rate of growth is about 50 cm per year. *R. globosa* likes a temperate to warm summer, with high rainfall.

Sapium integerrimum
Duiker-berry

Size: 3–5 x 3–5 m (wild), up to 4 x 4 m (garden)
Natural habitat: *Sapium* is confined to the coastal strip of KwaZulu-Natal and the Eastern Cape. It is found in many wooded habitats but is most common in coastal lowland forest, especially on the margins, and in small forest clumps in grassland. *Sapium* is an early coloniser of cleared land.
Growth form: It is a small tree with a chunky crown. The leaves have a bluish under-surface and delicate net-veining. The flowers are yellow, and although tiny, are massed in spikes, arranged neatly and alternately along the twigs, producing a nice display. *Sapium* has pretty fruits: miniature red pumpkins, which adorn the tree like Christmas decorations. After falling, they blacken and split open in spring. The seeds resemble miniature birds' eggs. They have a cream background, and are spotted and streaked with black.
Propagation: Seed.
Uses: *Sapium* makes a nice little form specimen after about five years. Fruiting begins then within the natural range, but has not so far been observed outside it. Speed of growth is moderate, about 50 cm per year, provided that the summer is warm and rainfall good. *Sapium* withstands moderate drought, but is frost-sensitive.

The indigenous garden Wholly indigenous gardens are not as modern a concept as is generally supposed. In the fifteenth century, the Aztec Montezuma I, an ancestor of the last and famous king of that name, created a garden entirely from the wild plants surrounding his palace.

Schotia brachypetala
Weeping boer-bean

Size: 4–12 x 5–15 m (wild), up to 7 x 9 m (garden)
Natural habitat: *Schotia* occurs naturally in the warm, deciduous woodlands of the east.
Growth form: *Schotia* can be thickset and craggy, or large and spreading. The canopy is dense and evergreen, although thinning a little in winter. Emerging new leaves are orange-brown. The flowers are outstanding, glorious deep red, and can cover the tree in September. In a good year, splashes of red dot the countryside when the rest of the veld is brown and tired. The flowers are not tubular, but cup-shaped, so that the copious supply of nectar is accessible to all birds, not just to sunbirds. Up to 15 different species of bird visit a flowering tree at once. Woody pods follow, tending to disintegrate while still on the tree, revealing pale pinkish-brown seeds, each with a small waxy yellow nodule attached to the seed. This is the host plant of the butterfly *Charaxes jasius*.
Propagation: Seed, which can be stored.
Uses: *Schotia* is ideal in a bird garden. It is worth growing for the flowers alone, and eventually makes a perfect shade tree. First flowering occurs at five years. Growth rate averages 40 cm per year. It grows best where summers are hot and rainfall low to moderate. It tolerates high rainfall.

Schrebera alata
Wild jasmine

Size: 3–8 x 2–6 m (wild), up to 6 x 4 m (garden)
Natural habitat: *Schrebera* is found naturally in the warmer parts of the east and north. It occurs on forest fringes, and especially on cliff edges and steep rocky slopes.
Growth form: It is a small, erect tree, although it often branches low down. The leaves are compound and divided, and very unusual; the stalk bears narrow, sweeping wings. Although evergreen, this tree never has dense foliage, and there is a thin period in a dry winter. *Schrebera* has lovely flowers, reminiscent of jasmine, sweet-smelling white trumpets with a pale pink centre. The fruits are also attractive and highly adapted for wind dispersal. They are little woody clubs that split when mature to release the papery seeds.
Propagation: Seed. The trick is to intercept the fruit just before it splits and scatters the seeds.
Uses: *Schrebera* makes a worthwhile flowering specimen, or it could be used on the sunny fringe of a forest clump, where its leaves would add greatly to foliage texture. First flowering takes place at two years in full sunshine. Growth is rapid, about 80 cm per year. *Schrebera* likes a temperate to warm summer, with moderate to good rainfall. It survives moderate drought and slight frost.

Why red? Red flowers owe their colour to anthocyanins, pigments that turn red in acid cell sap, and birds are the target audience. To ensure they are properly pollinated, these flowers have evolved to attract a specialised group of birds, so much so that the birds have become partially dependent upon the flowers.

Sclerocarya birrea
Maroela

Size: 7–15 x 8–20 m (wild), up to 9 x 12 m (garden)
Natural habitat: The maroela is found almost throughout the warmer parts of the east. This tree is most typically a major component of deciduous woodland.
Growth form: The maroela is a large, spreading tree that casts good shade in summer. New growth in spring is metallic red, and, in dry areas, autumn leaves turn yellow. Small, stiff flowering spikes emerge in early spring. The fruits begin developing in late spring and are mature around Christmas. In a good year the crop can be so heavy that the branches actually hang under the weight. Usually, most of the fruits fall while still green, only ripening and turning yellow on the ground. Most mammals enjoy them, especially fruit bats, elephants and warthogs. 
Propagation: Seed or cuttings.
Uses: The maroela makes an ideal shade or specimen tree. First flowering occurs at four years. Only female trees bear fruit. These are among the tastiest of all wild fruits and can be made into a superb jelly. Growth rate is about 70 cm per year, given a warm summer and frost-free winter.

Scolopia mundii
Red pear

Size: 8–20 x 7–18 m (wild), up to 10 x 9 m (garden)
Natural habitat: *Scolopia* ranges from the southwestern Cape through KwaZulu-Natal to the eastern Escarpment. It is locally common in evergreen forest, especially in cooler parts of the mist-belt and at fairly high altitudes.
Growth form: The growth form is upright. Young trees bear spines, but these are usually lost at maturity. Older trees have a fluted trunk. The foliage is dense, the leaves glossy and leathery. The flowers are insignificant but the fruits can be spectacular. They are large, bright yellow berries produced in mid-winter. This makes them an important resource for birds in cold areas at a time when little other fruit is available.
Propagation: Seed, although germination rate is poor.
Uses: *Scolopia* eventually makes a fine specimen and provides good screening and background foliage in its youth. It is ideal for a bird garden in cool damp areas. Fruiting has been noted at three years, although five years is more typical. Growth rate after planting out is fairly slow, about 30 cm per year. *Scolopia* can be grown in a wide range of different climatic conditions. This tree grows best in high rainfall, but withstands moderate drought.

Making jams and jellies Indigenous fruits make delicious jellies and jams. Experiment with maroela (*Sclerocarya birrea*), *Dovyalis longispina*, and *Ximenia caffra*, and create unique gifts. Your family will enjoy these tasty confections.

Securidaca longipedunculata
Violet tree

Size: 4–7 x 3–5 m (wild), up to 4 x 3 m (garden)
Natural habitat: *Securidaca* is found in the drier, warmer parts of the northeast. This tree occurs in deciduous woodland, especially on sandy soil, but is never dominant.
Growth form: It is upright, with a fairly narrow crown. The trunk is smooth, almost snow-white, and visible from afar when the veld is bare. Young plants have rambling, spiny branches. The flowers are pea-shaped and pale purple, and cover the leafless tree in spring. Good displays occur about one year in three. The fruit bears a papery wing, maple-style. 
Propagation: Seed. Seedlings grow best in a sandy mixture but do not last long in a pot. However, if planted out in a dry, sandy spot the young tree grows well enough. Results improve if soil from its natural range is mixed in the growing medium.
Uses: This tree has been little cultivated. A specimen planted in Johannesburg flowered after 12 years despite being frosted back repeatedly. No doubt it would have performed better in a warm climate more akin to the environment of its natural range. *Securidaca* probably would not thrive in high rainfall.

Sideroxylon inerme
White milkwood

Size: 5–9 x 7–13 m (wild), up to 7 x 10 m (garden)
Natural habitat: *Sideroxylon* is predominantly a coastal species, ranging from the Western Cape to KwaZulu-Natal, just extending into the eastern Lowveld. It is common on coastal dunes, lowland forest, and in deciduous woodland.
Growth form: It is a densely evergreen tree, with a heavy, spreading canopy. Dune specimens tend to be bent into interesting shapes by sea winds which damage growing points. The bark of older trees is almost black and fissured in a rectangular pattern. The leaves are dark and glossy. *Sideroxylon* is noted for its fruiting displays. The fruits are large, black, juicy berries greatly loved by birds, especially parrots and hornbills, and by fruit bats.
Propagation: Seed.
Uses: *Sideroxylon* makes a good screen if plenty of space is available and is especially useful next to a windy beach. With a little pruning it eventually makes a good shade tree and is ideal for a bird garden. First fruiting occurs at about three years, even outside the natural range. Growth rate is modest, about 40 cm per year. Good performance can be expected in a warm or temperate summer with moderate to good rainfall. *Sideroxylon* survives slight frost.

Pruning your trees When pruning your trees, cut flush with the trunk. Don't leave ugly stumps sticking out. Not only are they unattractive, but they will probably also sprout from the base again.

Spirostachys africana
Tamboti

Size: 6–11 x 5–11 m (wild), up to 9 x 8 m (garden)
Natural habitat: The tamboti is found in the warmer parts of the east. It occurs in deciduous woodland, sometimes in impressive single-species stands, often lining watercourses.
Growth form: It is upright and slender when young; in later life it has a dense rounded crown. On mature trees the bark is almost black and cracks into neat rectangles. Autumn colours begin with yellow leaves in May, but, as winter progresses, red dominates. Flowering takes place in mid-winter. The whole tree becomes covered with pinkish-brown catkins, with glossy, tightly overlapping scales. At maturity these emit puffs of yellow pollen when the tree is shaken. The fruits are dry capsules, entertaining when they split explosively, scattering the seed.
Propagation: Seed or cuttings.
Uses: This is a good shade tree, and a must for bark and autumn colour fanciers. These colours develop best in dry winters. If space permits, plant a group of three, with a spacing of 5–7 m. This provides the cool shade of a wild grove. Growth rate is 1 m per year, given a warm summer, slight frost and moderate rainfall. Tambotis make good bonsais.

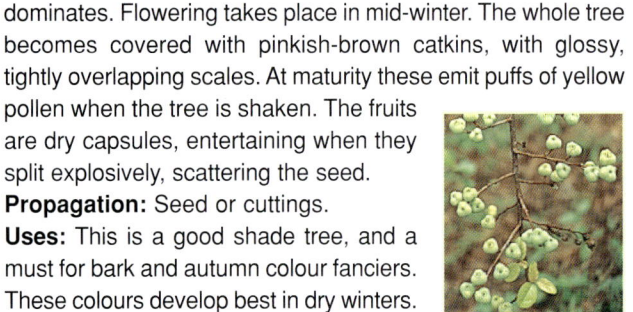

Steganotaenia araliacea
Carrot tree

Size: 4–9 x 2–5 m (wild), up to 6 x 4 m (garden)
Natural habitat: This tree is found in the Lowveld, and is most common on koppies. Some large specimens can be seen on the hill beside Masorini Museum in the Kruger National Park.
Growth form: It is thin and upright. It can be recognised from some distance by its bark. This is smooth and pale yellow-grey, peels in papery layers and gleams in bright sunshine. *Steganotaenia* has unusual and attractive leaves. These are compound, being divided into leaflets with heavily toothed edges. Crushed leaves smell of carrots. The flowers are white, and, although small, they appear much bigger, as they grow clustered together in large spherical flowering heads when the tree is leafless.
Propagation: Getting cuttings to grow is so easy that seed is rarely collected.
Uses: This tree makes an interesting and pretty specimen, which does not take up much space and is ideal for a hot, dry garden or a steep north-facing slope. The bark develops its typical colour and peel at about three years. Speed of growth is rewarding, about 80 cm per year. *Steganotaenia* is exceptionally drought-hardy, yet tolerates high rainfall, provided that drainage is good. It also survives some frost.

Indigenous firewood When taking off large branches, cut them up for firewood. It is a wonderful talking point being able to identify your logs by name. Just be careful of trees such as the tamboti, *Spirostachys africana*, whose wood gives off semi-poisonous smoke. Obviously, this tree should not to be used as firewood.

Sterculia murex
Lowveld chestnut

Size: 5–8 x 6–9 m (wild), up to 10 x 10 m (garden)
Natural habitat: *S. murex* is a very localised species, being confined to the southeastern Lowveld, where it is invariably found on koppies or rocky hillsides.
Growth form: This tree has a slender, upright form when young, only developing a canopy in later life. The leaves are unusual, large and palmately compound. Flowers appear in great bunches in early spring when the tree is usually leafless. They are shallow, yellow cups, with orange markings inside. The fruits are even more spectacular, the woody shell being adorned with blunt spines. The fruits are grouped into clusters, which look like starfish. When mature, they split neatly and symmetrically into halves. Inside, the fruit is a large hollow, with the seeds, which resemble fat black ticks, lining up around the split edge of the fruit.
Propagation: Seed.
Uses: *S. murex* makes a fantastic specimen, worth prime place, and a reasonable shade tree after six years. Flowering begins at five years. Growth rate is about 70 cm per year. This tree likes a warm summer with moderate rainfall. It tolerates fairly high rainfall provided that drainage is good. The empty halves of the fruits make interesting ashtrays or ornaments.

Sterculia rogersii
Common star-chestnut

Size: 3–6 x 3–5 m (wild), up to 4 x 4 m (garden)
Natural habitat: *S. rogersii* is restricted to the Lowveld. It is found in dry, open woodland, often on rocky outcrops.
Growth form: It is short and thickset, the trunk frequently forking near the ground, and sometimes contorting into interesting shapes. The bark is a beautiful pale grey, peeling in patches to reveal a mosaic of yellow and bronze-red. A long deciduous period enhances these colours in a bright, dry winter. The flowers are yellow cups, heavily orange-streaked inside. The woody fruits are produced in clusters and have a velvet finish. When mature they split neatly into two halves. Inside, the fruit is hollow, with the seeds, which resemble fat black ticks, lining up around the split edge of the fruit.
Propagation: Seed.
Uses: *S. rogersii* makes a fantastic specimen. The north face of a rockery is ideal for it. Flowering begins at three years and by then the trunk is already developing a squat shape and its brilliant peeling colours. *S. rogersii* likes a dry spot; it can be killed by over-watering. Growth rate is about 30 cm per year, provided that the summer is warm, rainfall moderate and winters frost-free. The empty halves of the fruits are dry and make interesting ashtrays or ornaments.

Why yellow? Yellow flowers owe their colour to xanthophyll, although deeper shades verging on orange are the result of carotene. Bees are the main pollinators of yellow flowers, which often have red or purple markings to direct the bees straight to the pollen.

Strychnos decussata
Cape teak, Chaka's wood

Size: 5–12 x 5–10 m (wild), up to 9 x 8 m (garden)
Natural habitat: This species ranges from the Eastern Cape through the coastal regions of KwaZulu-Natal to the eastern Lowveld. It is found in coastal and sand forests, and dense deciduous woodland.
Growth form: *S. decussata* is an upright, elegant tree with a clean trunk and, in later life, a spreading crown. The leaves are glossy and neat. The fruits are small compared with those of other *Strychnos* species, 1.5 cm in diameter, and bitter to taste. These fruits are a beautiful bright orange, resembling small apricots, and may festoon the tree. Birds and antelopes eat them.
Propagation: Seed. Germination is best at 30 °C. It occurs far more slowly at lower temperatures.
Uses: When small, *S. decussata* makes a pretty specimen, eventually becoming an adequate, but not overwhelming, shade tree. Fruiting begins at about six years. Growth rate is modest, about 40 cm per year, provided the climate is warm and rainfall moderate to good. It tolerates moderate drought, but is probably not frost-hardy.

Strychnos spinosa
Spiny monkey orange

Size: 3–7 x 3–6 m (wild), up to 5 x 5 m (garden)
Natural habitat: *S. spinosa* ranges from the Eastern Cape through KwaZulu-Natal to the far northeast. It is widespread and common in deciduous woodland.
Growth form: It is a small, spiny tree with a spreading but sparse crown. The leaves are neat and glossy, with a distinctive forking vein pattern. The fruits adorn the tree for months and are well known to game reserve visitors. They are up to 12 cm in diameter and have a tough, woody shell. They are green when young, maturing to pale greenish-yellow, and are eaten by antelopes once they have fallen. Nyalas chew up the whole fruit, shell, pips and all. The pulp has an off-putting greyish colour but is delicious – worth serving at an avant-garde dinner.
Propagation: Seed. Germination is best at 30 °C, occurring much more slowly at lower temperatures.
Uses: *S. spinosa* is worth growing as an interesting small specimen. Fruiting begins at about six years. Growth is slow, about 30 cm per year. *S. spinosa* likes a warm summer, with moderate rainfall. It withstands slight frost. Although the fruits appear tough and long-lasting, they are not, and soon rot and collapse in dried flower arrangements.

Effective treatment for borer beetle Borer is the only pest that needs chemical treatment. Either cut off the affected part of the branch, including a bit of the unaffected wood closer to the trunk, to make sure you have removed all the borer bettle, or inject an approved insecticide directly into the offending bug hole.

Suregada zanzibariensis
Woodland suregada

Size: 2–5 x 2–4 m (wild), up to 4 x 3 m (garden)
Natural habitat: This species is restricted to northern Zululand. It occurs in the understorey of sand and dune forests.
Growth form: It is a slender, upright, evergreen tree, with regularly spaced horizontal branches. *Suregada* has elegant foliage, the leaves being leathery and glossy, with a 'pigskin' stipple to the surface. It is prettiest when in fruit. The fruits grow regularly lined up along every branch. They are three-lobed capsules that split at maturity to reveal orange seeds. Birds eat them.
Propagation: Seed.
Uses: *Suregada* is greatly recommended as a small specimen. Fruiting begins at seven years outside the natural range, and is prolific. *Suregada* is one of the few trees that grow well in half shade, although it would probably be equally happy in full sun. The young tree grows about 50 cm per year, given a warm summer with good rainfall. It is probably sensitive to frost.

Syzygium cordatum
Umdoni

Size: 9–15 x 10–17 m (wild), up to 11 x 13 m (garden)
Natural habitat: The umdoni is common in the warmer parts of the east. It often dominates swamp forest or river banks. It also grows on rocky outcrops.
Growth form: The umdoni is a large tree, with a heavy, rounded crown. It has dense foliage, which has a pleasant scent when crushed. The flowers are conspicuous white pompons, consisting mainly of stamens. They are sweetly scented and attract all manner of insects, particularly brightly coloured beetles. The fruits are large, dark, purple berries, relished by birds, especially green pigeons. Bats and people love them too. This is the host plant of the butterflies *Charaxes druceanus* and *Deudorix dinochares*.
Propagation: Seed, which must be very fresh. Viability is greatly reduced after as few as three days.
Uses: The umdoni makes a good shade tree and is ideal in a wildlife garden. Flowering and fruiting begin at about four years and fruits are produced outside the natural range, in Cape Town for example. The umdoni makes an adequate street or car park tree, where waterlogged ground excludes alternatives. Growth rate is about 60 cm per year. It likes a warm summer and high rainfall, but tolerates slight frost.

Waterlogging Waterlogging causes a lack of aeration in the soil. Under normal circumstances up to 50% of the soil consists of air spaces. These provide vital oxygen to tree roots. Even a high water table restricts tree growth by confining roots to the surface layers where air is present.

Tabernaemontana elegans
Toad tree

Size: 3–8 x 3–7 m (wild), up to 5 x 5 m (garden)
Natural habitat: This is a species of the Lowveld, where it occurs in deciduous woodland, often on sandy soil.
Growth form: *T. elegans* is a short, stocky tree. The bark is thickly corky. The leaves are large, dark and glossy. *T. elegans* is deciduous and can be spectacular in autumn, because the leaves turn yellow, while retaining their gloss. The flowers are twisted white stars, with a waxy texture and a sweet smell. They appear in masses in mid-summer. The fruit is large and striking, a twinned grey-green structure, covered with corky spots. It has a fair resemblance to a grinning toad when it splits at maturity. Once exposed, the mixture of orange pulp and dark seeds is rapidly consumed by birds and fruit bats. 
Propagation: Seed, which must be fresh.
Uses: This tree makes a brilliant small specimen. In cultivation it rarely loses all its leaves. It flowers at three years, prolifically by five. Fruiting occurs outside the natural range, but not with the abandon typical of its natural haunts. Growth rate is about 50 cm per year. It likes a warm summer and moderate rainfall.

Tabernaemontana ventricosa
Forest toad tree

Size: 4–9 x 3–7 m (wild), up to 6 x 5 m (garden)
Natural habitat: *T. ventricosa* is found in the KwaZulu-Natal coastal strip and in parts of the eastern Lowveld. It occurs in evergreen forest, either in the understorey or on the margin.
Growth form: It is a small, slender, elegant tree. The bark is smooth. The leaves are large, dark and glossy, giving the foliage a tropical look. The flowers are large and white, with a waxy texture and a sweet smell, and they are star-shaped, with a spiral twist. The fruit is large and striking, a twinned structure, mottled various shades of polished green, with a fair resemblance to a grinning toad when it splits at maturity. Once exposed, the mixture of orange pulp and dark seeds is rapidly consumed by birds and fruit bats.
Propagation: Seed, which must be fresh.
Uses: *T. ventricosa* makes a brilliant small specimen. It flowers at four years, more prolifically in full sun. Rate of growth is moderate, about 50 cm per year. It thrives in full sun or partial shade, provided that the summer is warm, rainfall is high and the winter frost-free.

Seeds from the veld Collect the seeds of your favourite veld trees. This is free of charge and rewarding. In most cases there is no legal restriction, other than obtaining the landowner's permission. Seed collecting at this level does not harm the reproductive success of the wild population.

Tarchonanthus camphoratus
Camphor bush, Vaalbos

Size: 3–6 x 2–5 m (wild), up to 5 x 4 m (garden)
Natural habitat: *Tarchonanthus* is widespread, being absent from only the driest deserts and the highest mountain tops. It is most common in dry scrub and deciduous woodland.
Growth form: It can be a well-shaped tree or an erect shrub. The corky bark is attractively fissured. The leaves are a muted greyish-green, with off-white under-surfaces. Both crushed leaves and broken branches are famous for their camphor smell. *Tarchonanthus* is variably deciduous, depending upon the severity of winter. The leaves turn yellow in a dry autumn. The cream-coloured flowers are small and thistle-like. The fruits are tiny and produced on the female trees in a mass of woolly hairs resembling cotton wool. They are wind dispersed.
Propagation: Seed.
Uses: *Tarchonanthus* makes a nice specimen after four years. It is worth growing for its form, bark and foliage. Growth is moderately fast, about 70 cm per year. This species can be cultivated almost anywhere, and is especially useful where drought and frost kill nearly everything else.

Terminalia phanerophlebia
Lebombo cluster-leaf

Size: 4–8 x 3–7 m (wild), up to 10 x 9 m (garden)
Natural habitat: This species is restricted to woodlands and rocky hillsides in the eastern Lowveld.
Growth form: It is erect, with a pagoda growth form, the branches growing in horizontal layers. The bark of young trees is finely fissured, revealing the orange underbark. The foliage turns a delicate mixture of pink and yellow in autumn. The flowers are white catkins. The fruits are flat, with two wings, and a dark pink or maroon centre. This hue diffuses towards the wings when the fruit matures in late autumn, as the leaves change colour. On any one tree, large numbers of fruit will grow orientated in the same direction, so that when they catch the sun the colours are intensified.
Propagation: Germination of seemingly good wild seed is very poor. Seed from trees cultivated outside the natural habitat germinates far better.
Uses: *T. phanerophlebia* is a wonderful shade and form tree. The pagoda habit develops within two years. First flowering and fruiting occur at four years. Growth rate is about 70 cm a year, given a warm summer.

Tree scents Every plant has a unique smell. Aromatic leaves add an extra dimension to the garden, with scents of lemon, myrtle, lavender, curry, carrot and camphor, plus others not so easily defined. *Heteropyxis natalensis* and *Tarchonanthus camphoratus* are two of the best-scented trees.

Terminalia prunioides
Lowveld cluster-leaf

Size: 4–7 x 3–6 m (wild), up to 4 x 4 m (garden)
Natural habitat: This species is restricted to dry woodlands in the far northeast.
Growth form: It is a small, compact tree, easily recognised by its shape. The branches are regularly curved, usually bending in a half-circle and touching the ground. The bark is pretty, narrowly fissured to reveal orange underbark. The flowers are attractive, white and grow in catkin-like spikes. The two-winged fruits are exceptionally pretty. The crop is always heavy and begins maturing in mid-summer. Ripe fruits are deep maroon and cover the tree until mid-winter. 
Propagation: Germination of seemingly perfect wild seed is very poor. Seeds taken from trees cultivated outside the natural range germinate much better.
Uses: This tree makes a distinctive small specimen. Its ability to flower and fruit outside its natural habitat has yet to be proved. Growth is fairly slow, about 40 cm per year. Best results can be expected where the summer is warm and rainfall moderate to low. Light frost is tolerated.

Terminalia sericea
Vaalboom

Size: 4–10 x 4–10 m (wild), up to 8 x 7 m (garden)
Natural habitat: T. sericea is locally common in the warm, dry parts of the east and north, particularly where the soil is sandy.
Growth form: It is an upright tree that develops a spreading canopy towards maturity. The bark is neatly fissured, in a zigzag pattern, on older trees. T. sericea's leaves have an exceptionally fine colour; they are a blend of blue, green and pale grey, recalling the silver trees on the slopes of Table Mountain. They are covered with a layer of reflective hairs causing the whole tree to shimmer in bright sunlight. The two-winged fruits mature to a pale pink colour, the pink blush beginning at the edge of the wings and diffusing inwards.
Propagation: Germination of seemingly perfect wild seed is very poor. Seeds taken from trees cultivated outside the natural range germinate much better, and results are further improved if the wings are cut off the fruits before sowing.
Uses: T. sericea makes a fine specimen for a prime position, and adds a new dimension in colour and texture to the garden. Flowering and fruiting begin at three years, even outside the natural range. The ideal is a warm summer, with moderate to low rainfall. Sandy soil is not essential, but is an asset in a wet climate. Growth is rapid, 1 m per year.

Cutting your losses If a tree you have planted is battling with your conditions and needs constant protection and special treatment, consider starting again with a species better suited to your environment.

Thespesia acutiloba
Wild tulip tree

Size: 3–5 x 2–4 m (wild), up to 4 x 3 m (garden)
Natural habitat: *Thespesia* is confined to Zululand. It occurs in deciduous woodland, especially in thickets on termite mounds or on evergreen forest fringes.
Growth form: It is a fairly small tree with a tendency to be multi-stemmed. The leaves have a pleasing and distinctive heart shape, resembling ivy. *Thespesia* has very pretty flowers. Their shape reveals a relationship with *Hibiscus*. The petals are yellow and quite large, and overlap to form a flaring trumpet. Inside the trumpet, the base is deep maroon. The fruits are red and fleshy, 1.2 cm in diameter. They are very popular with all wildlife, and it is difficult to find more than one or two ripe fruits on any tree.
Propagation: Seed or cuttings.
Uses: *Thespesia* can be used both as a flowering and a foliage specimen, or as part of an informal screen. It does, however, lose its leaves for up to two months in a dry winter. Flowering begins at four years. A warm, sunny spot and moderate rainfall give best results. Growth rate is about 60 cm per year. *Thespesia* tolerates some frost.

Trema orientalis
Pigeonwood

Size: 6–13 x 5–11 m (wild), up to 10 x 9 m (garden)
Natural habitat: *Trema* is found in the warm, damp parts of the east. It is a forest dweller but develops best if always exposed to full sun. So, it is most common at forest edges, and particularly as a pioneer in newly cleared forest.
Growth form: It is a large tree with a broad canopy. The foliage is popular with small caterpillars and other insects, and, therefore, insectivorous birds. *Trema* always has a dead branch somewhere, of interest to woodpeckers and barbets. The black berries, although tiny, are produced in abundance and make a pretty display. *Trema* is a wonderful bird tree. It begins fruiting at two years and attracts all fruit-eaters.
Propagation: Seed, often planted by visiting birds.
Uses: *Trema* is the fastest-growing of all indigenous trees, gaining at least 2 m per year – perfect where instant shade is required. It is semi-deciduous, the degree of leaf-fall depending upon the severity of the winter. Try leaving the area beneath a *Trema* canopy uncut, and watch developments. All manner of things will spring up, all brought by birds. In the wild, *Trema* provides the ideal shelter for young forest trees that like half shade. So to re-establish a natural forest on a large plot, plant a grove of *Trema*. It likes good rainfall and a warm climate.

Nesting opportunities Keep a dead tree, or even a dead branch on a live tree. These provide vital nesting opportunities for hole-nesting birds such as woodpeckers and barbets.

Trichilia emetica
Natal mahogany, Umkhuhlu

Size: 7–20 x 6–20 m (wild), up to 15 x 15 m (garden)
Natural habitat: This species ranges from the KwaZulu-Natal coast to the eastern Lowveld. *Trichilia* is sometimes found in evergreen forest, but is more common in riverine fringes in deciduous woodland.
Growth form: *Trichilia* is a large, imposing tree, with a broad canopy that casts dense shade. The leaves are handsome, large, and very dark. The flowers are an extremely pale green, almost white, and produced in tight bunches on terminal twigs. They have a sweet smell and attract bees. The fruits are striking. They are round capsules that split when mature, revealing bright red-and-black seeds. Despite their large size, these are swallowed whole by tiny tinker barbets. Hornbills and fruit bats like them too. Eventually the remaining seeds are shed, forming a colourful carpet beneath the tree.
Propagation: Seed, which must be fresh.
Uses: *Trichilia* makes a perfect shade tree from four years onwards, eventually becoming big enough for car parks and avenues. Fruiting first occurs at about six years, although cannot be guaranteed. A few trees bear only male flowers, so will never fruit. Growth is rapid, 1 m per year, if the summer is warm and rainfall high. *Trichilia* withstands slight frost.

Trichocladus grandiflorus
Green witch-hazel

Size: 5–8 x 4–6 m (wild), up to 4 x 3 m (garden)
Natural habitat: This tree ranges from southern KwaZulu-Natal through the mist-belt escarpments to the far northeast. It is confined to coastal and mist-belt forests.
Growth form: It is always erect and slender. It is noted for its exceptionally attractive foliage. The leaves are elegantly veined, long and slim, with the tip drawn out into a fine point. New growth is bronze-red. The flowers are exquisite, with long thin petals massed into ragged, spherical heads. The petals are white and crinkly, with a deep pink base. Flowering takes place in summer.
Propagation: Seed or cuttings.
Uses: *Trichocladus* is particularly attractive, worth growing for both foliage and flowers, and is especially useful because it looks its best in half shade. Flowering begins at about five years. Growth in cultivation is quick, up to 1 m per year. This tree demands high rainfall, but grows equally well in a warm or temperate summer. It is one of the few trees that actually dislikes full sunshine, and it is sensitive to drought and frost.

The origin of trees Trees have a wonderful history. Their lineage began 380 million years ago with the appearance of the ancestors of modern cycads and tree ferns. Many modern trees attain great age and outlive human beings. A baobab may live for 2,000 years or more.

Trimeria grandifolia
Big ears

Size: 3–7 x 2–5 m (wild), up to 4 x 3 m (garden)
Natural habitat: *Trimeria* ranges from the southern Cape, through KwaZulu-Natal, to the eastern Escarpment. It occurs in evergreen forests, often at the margins or in the understorey.
Growth form: The growth form is very graceful, slender and upright, with horizontal branches arranged in layers. The foliage complements this form and emphasises the tree's profile, as the leaves are also held horizontally. The leaves are a bright fresh green, large and rounded, with all the main veins radiating directly from the leaf base. The fruits grow on the female trees. They are small and yellow, and sought-after by bulbuls and tinker barbets.
Propagation: Seed.
Uses: *Trimeria* is a fine form and foliage tree that does not take up much space. The tree grows well in partial shade, but grows at least as well in full sun, an environment rarely encountered in the veld. There, in the wild, it fruits at about four years. In cultivation, the tree does not begin fruiting until it is about eight years old. Growth is rapid, about 80 cm per year. It likes a warm or temperate summer, with good rainfall. Drought tolerance is slight, frost resistance moderate.

Turraea floribunda
Wild honeysuckle tree

Size: 3–9 x 2–6 m (wild), up to 5 x 3 m (garden)
Natural habitat: This species is found naturally in the warm, wetter parts of the Eastern Cape and KwaZulu-Natal. It occurs in coastal forest and in deciduous woodland, provided there are rocks to protect it from fire.
Growth form: It is a slender tree, or upright shrub, which leans on its neighbours. The leaves have neat herringbone veins. The flowers are very beautiful, creamy white, with long, thin, slightly twisted petals. They have a sweet smell, and superficially resemble the flowers of the ordinary honeysuckle. They appear in early summer, when great sprays cascade from the forest edge. The fruit is green, even when mature. On a dry day, when the fruit is ripe, it splits, and the outer casing peels back, revealing a tightly packed mass of orange seeds. This is an obvious adaptation to attract birds.
Propagation: Seed.
Uses: *Turraea* makes a nice flowering and fruiting specimen, and is ideal for a bird garden. It is best grown in a mixed, tall shrubbery, or against a fence, where unruly branches can be accommodated. First flowering occurs at about four years. Growth rate is about 80 cm per year, given a warm summer with moderate to high rainfall.

Seed coatings Seeds with hard coatings, such as those of *Acacia*, are encouraged to germinate by having boiling water poured over them and then being left in the water for 24 hours, until they swell. Big, hard seeds benefit from some roughening with a metal file.

Vangueria infausta
Wild medlar

Size: 2–5 x 2–4 m (wild), up to 3 x 3 m (garden)
Natural habitat: *Vangueria* is found over most of the northeast, and in the warmer parts of KwaZulu-Natal. It occurs in deciduous woodland, especially in rocky areas, and in sandy soil in coastal grassland.
Growth form: It is a small, thickset tree, sometimes shrubby. The bark is smooth and pale yellowish-grey, and stands out in winter sunshine when the tree is leafless. The leaves are very large and thickly furry. The flowers are white and fairly small, but sweetly scented and delicately formed. The fruits are orange and quite large. They are eaten by all animals – even tortoises join the feast and have been seen ramming the trunks of small trees, in order to shake the fruits down. They have a pleasant, slightly sour, fruity flavour, and make a fair substitute for tamarind in curry.
Propagation: Seed.
Uses: Although *Vangueria* has no single outstanding quality, its combination of modest size, interesting bark and foliage, pretty flowers and bird-attracting fruits makes it well worth growing, either as a specimen, or on the sunny side of a bush clump in a bird garden. Flowering and fruiting begin at three years. Growth is fairly slow, about 40 cm per year.

Vepris lanceolata
White ironwood

Size: 5–25 x 4–20 m (wild), up to 10 x 9 m (garden)
Natural habitat: *Vepris* is fairly widespread over the wetter parts of the south, east and northeast of the country. It can be locally common in mist-belt and coastal forest, and also occurs sparingly in thornveld, among rocks.
Growth form: It is usually a large, imposing tree, taller than its spread is wide. The foliage is elegant, the leaves being glossy and divided into three leaflets. The leaves have a faint lemon smell when crushed. The flowers are white and tiny, growing in cauliflower-like heads, and make a brief show. The fruits are black berries, borne in great bunches, with birds in attendance. *Vepris* is host to the butterfly *Papilio dardanus*.
Propagation: Seed, often planted by visiting birds.
Uses: *Vepris* can be used as a shade tree, as background foliage, or as a useful component of a bird garden. It grows well enough in a beach garden, provided that a windbreak is present initially. Flowering and fruiting have occurred at three years, but five to eight years is more typical. Infestations of aphids sometimes appear on *Vepris*, but no harm seems to be done, and aphid-eating white-eyes are the chief beneficiaries. Growth rate is about 80 cm per year where rainfall is high and the soil good, considerably less in poor conditions.

Maximising sun Identify your north-facing boundary and be very careful not to plant large trees here, as they will cut out all the light and sun from the rest of the garden.

Vernonia colorata
Lowveld tree vernonia

Size: 3–5 x 3–5 m (wild), up to 4 x 3 m (garden)
Natural habitat: *Vernonia* is restricted to the warm southeast of the country where it occurs in deciduous woodland and in clearings in riverine forest.
Growth form: It is a shrubby but erect tree. The leaves are bright green and furry in texture. They are also incredibly wavy on a young plant, where the leaves are held horizontally, showing off the feature to best effect. In a dry winter, there may be a short deciduous period. *Vernonia* is noted for its flowering displays, which take place in autumn and early winter. The flowers are a pale mauve when they first open, fading to white after a few days. Numerous insects attend them, especially bees, butterflies and small, brightly coloured moths.
Propagation: Seed.
Uses: Because *Vernonia* is a bit scrappy in growth form, it is not an ideal specimen plant, but mixes well in shrubby thickets and it adds much to a wildlife garden. Flowering sometimes takes place in the first year, and it is profuse and reliable from the second year onwards. Growth is rapid, up to 1 m per year initially, slowing as the plant thickens out. *Vernonia* likes a warm summer, with moderate to good rainfall. Frost tolerance is unknown.

Virgilia divaricata
Keurboom

Size: 6–8 x 5–6 m (wild), up to 6 x 5 m (garden)
Natural habitat: *Virgilia* occurs in the coastal strip of the southern Cape, especially around Knysna. This tree is a forest precursor, usually being the first coloniser of a cleared area that is climatically suitable for evergreen forest.
Growth form: This tree is upright in form with a fairly dense canopy, which allows some sunlight through, creating ideal conditions for the germination of other forest trees. *Virgilia* has a short life, typically 6–12 years, and dies of old age when the secondary colonisers are well established beneath it. The flowers are very pretty, pea-shaped, and rich deep pink. They form massed displays, attended by carpenter bees.
Propagation: Seed.
Uses: *Virgilia* is the nearest thing to an instant tree in a new garden, but must be regarded as a temporary feature, and the garden planned accordingly. Indeed it sometimes seems to outgrow its strength and fall over, the root system being rather puny compared with the tree's above-ground weight. It makes a passable shade tree where speed is important. Flowering begins at two years. Growth is very rapid, sometimes 2 m per year. *Virgilia* must have high rainfall and a cool or temperate summer. It tolerates slight frost.

The right dose of fertiliser Indigenous trees do not enjoy too much fertiliser. An initial dose of superphosphate and 2.3.2 mixed into the soil when planting is sufficient. Additional fertiliser after this can be fatal.

Widdringtonia nodiflora
Berg cypress, Mountain cedar

Size: 5–7 x 3–5 m (wild), up to 4 x 3 m (garden)
Natural habitat: *Widdringtonia*, as both its common names suggest, occurs naturally in the mountains, ranging from the southwestern Cape, through the Drakensberg, to the eastern Escarpment. This tree is found only in sunny habitats that are protected from fire, usually among rocks. A particularly fine community can be seen at Giant's Castle, in the Drakensberg.
Growth form: *Widdringtonia* is a slender and upright tree, with a narrow conical shape, strongly resembling other small, evergreen conifers so widely used in formal gardening. Leaf form varies with age. On young plants the leaves are needle-like, only being replaced with the minute leaves of mature trees after eight years or so. Bruised leaves smell of resin. Grey cones are produced in masses along the smaller branches. When mature they split to reveal flat, black, winged seeds, tightly packed together.
Propagation: Seed.
Uses: Growth rate is slow, about 30 cm per year. This is not necessarily a disadvantage, for it enables *Widdringtonia* to be used as a miniature specimen. Its size also makes this tree a good container plant. *Widdringtonia* grows best in a cool or temperate climate with good rainfall.

Wrightia natalensis
Saddle pod

Size: 3–8 x 2–6 m (wild), up to 5 x 4 m (garden)
Natural habitat: *Wrightia* ranges from the KwaZulu-Natal coast to the eastern Lowveld. It is common in sand forest and may be locally abundant in dense dry woodland.
Growth form: It is a small, upright tree, with a well-developed pagoda habit in which the branches tend to grow horizontally, in clearly defined layers. The leaves are pretty, being glossy, long and thin. The deciduous period lasts about four months. The flowers appear in early spring and are bright yellow, with a waxy texture. The fruit is remarkable, consisting of a pair of long, thin, pointed tubes, which split when mature, to release dandelion-like, parachute-assisted seeds.
Propagation: Seed.
Uses: *Wrightia* is well worth growing as a form, foliage and flowering specimen. The age of first flowering is about five years. Growth in cultivation is fairly slow, about 40 cm per year, but a pleasing little pagoda results after five years. It likes a warm summer, with moderate to low rainfall. Its frost tolerance is unknown, but likely to be slight at best. *Wrightia* makes a good bonsai.

Protecting your trees If you are lucky enough to have duiker and bushbuck in your garden, guard young trees with wire cages. Side branches that get nibbled are expendable – it's the leading shoot that matters. Keep mice and porcupines at bay with fine netting directly round the lower trunk.

Ximenia caffra
Large sourplum

Size: 3–6 x 3–5 m (wild), up to 3 x 3 m (garden)
Natural habitat: *Ximenia* is fairly widespread in the warmer parts of the east. It occurs in deciduous woodland, often among rocks or on termite mounds.
Growth form: It is a small tree, sometimes multi-stemmed, but always upright, with rigid, angular, spine-tipped branches. *Ximenia* produces spectacular crops of fruit in autumn. The fruits resemble small orange-red plums and have a sharp taste. Although a bit face-puckering by human standards, they make excellent jelly, provided that any have been spared by the birds. Only female trees bear fruit. *Ximenia* is the host of the butterfly *Iolaus pallene*.
Propagation: Seed, although subsequent growth in a pot is poor. *Ximenia* seems to be partly parasitic, growing far better once its roots come into contact with those of other species.
Uses: *Ximenia* is no horticultural beauty, but has rugged charm, and could be used as a barrier plant. It also mixes well with other deciduous, thorny trees and is ideal for a bird garden. Fruiting begins at about five years. Growth rate is approximately 50 cm per year. *Ximenia* grows best when the climate is warm and rainfall moderate. However, it tolerates a little frost, and high rainfall if drainage is good.

Xylotheca kraussiana
African dog-rose

Size: 3–8 x 3–6 m (wild), up to 4 x 3 m (garden)
Natural habitat: *Xylotheca* is common in coastal KwaZulu-Natal and rare in the eastern Lowveld. It is found on forest edges, in dune scrub and scattered in coastal grassland.
Growth form: It is a small, more or less evergreen tree or shrub. Its flowers and fruits are outstanding. The flowers are about 5 cm in diameter and have large white petals with a central yellow mass of stamens. They are sweetly scented. Individual flowers are quite long-lived, so the plant can be covered with flowers for up to two months. The fruits are woody capsules. They split when ripe and the drying segments of skin curl back to reveal the beautiful red-and-black seeds. Fruiting trees are besieged by birds until stripped. *Xylotheca* is host to the butterflies *Acraea petraea* and *A. oncaea*.
Propagation: Seed.
Uses: *Xylotheca* can be used as a good small specimen and, as it retains most of its lower branches, makes a good screen. It is essential in a bird garden. Flowering and fruiting commence in the second year, even well outside the species' natural habitat. Growth rate is 50 cm per year, given a warm summer, moderate to good rainfall, and frost-free winter. Old fruits harden into perfect stars and make lasting ornaments.

Gold and silver garden When the Caliph of old Baghdad wanted a bird garden he built a tree of gold whose fruits were precious stones. Gold and silver birds sat in the branches and whistled in the wind. But the observance of a few ecological principles will produce better results!

Xymalos monospora
Lemonwood

Size: 8–20 x 10–24 m (wild), up to 9 x 12 m (garden)
Natural habitat: *Xymalos* ranges from the Eastern Cape, through KwaZulu-Natal, to the eastern Escarpment. It is confined to evergreen forest, often dominating the mist-belt.
Growth form: The shape of the tree varies greatly with age. In its youth it is slender and erect, thickening out, with a good canopy, in early middle age. After this it sprouts again at the base, as the main trunk begins to rot, and eventually a circle of new trunks grows to surround the hollow space left by the original trunk. The bark is unique. As the outer layers flake off, they reveal remarkable spiral patterns beneath. *Xymalos* has attractive foliage. The leaves are deep green with a quilted texture. The fruits resemble small plums and grow only on female trees. They are reputedly red when ripe, but birds intercept them when they are still greenish-orange.
Propagation: Seed or cuttings.
Uses: *Xymalos* makes a good foliage tree. Under garden conditions it tends to retain its lower branches, so is better used in the background than as a shade tree. Fruiting begins at six years. Rate of growth is about 50 cm per year. It likes a cool to temperate summer with good rainfall, but can tolerate warmth if rainfall is high enough. It survives moderate frost.

Zanthoxylum capense
Small knobwood

Size: 3–10 x 2–7 m (wild), up to 5 x 3 m (garden)
Natural habitat: *Z. capense* ranges from the southern Cape along a broad coastal strip to Zululand, and then northwards. It is found in dry woodland, often in hot rocky places.
Growth form: It is usually small and slender, branching low down. The trunk has spines, strong and sharp on the young tree, growing into pyramidal knobs later. *Z. capense*'s leaves are glossy and divided. The fruits are produced in clusters, turning dull red when mature and splitting to reveal shiny black seeds. *Z. capense* belongs to the citrus family, and both leaves and fruits have a strong, even overwhelming, lemon smell and taste. Even so, birds eat the seeds. It is the host plant of the butterflies *Papilio echerioides* and *P. ophidicephalus*.
Propagation: Seed is often parasitised and germination in cultivation is usually poor. However, there are often plenty of spare seedlings to be harvested beneath wild trees.
Uses: *Z. capense* is well worth growing for its foliage, its trunk, unique to its genus, and to attract birds. Fruits first appear at about three years. Growth rate is about 70 cm per year. It likes a warm summer with moderate rainfall. An interesting home-made 'gin' can be produced by soaking half-crushed green fruits in cane spirits.

Tree defences Spines evolved as a defence against large browsers. It is interesting to note that non-spiny trees either have chemicals distasteful to mammals and insects in their leaves or are deciduous and thus make good their losses within a season. Older trees bear relatively few spines.

Zanthoxylum davyi
Knobwood

Size: 10–20 x 6–13 m (wild), up to 9 x 6 m (garden)
Natural habitat: *Z. davyi* occurs in the wetter parts of the east, and is found in coastal and mist-belt forests.
Growth form: It is single-stemmed and slender. Strong sharp spines grow on the young trunk. These grow throughout the tree's life, so that the long unbranched trunks of older trees are dominated by massed spines, each up to 3 cm long, and pyramidal in shape. This remarkable sight, not unusual in equatorial forests, confers a tropical air to the cool forests of the mist-belt. The fruits are produced in clusters, turning dull red when mature and splitting open to reveal shiny black seeds. *Z. davyi* belongs to the citrus family and both leaves and fruits have a strong, even overwhelming, lemon smell and taste. This does not deter the birds that seek out the seeds.
Propagation: Seed is often parasitised, and germination in cultivation is usually poor. However, germination under a parent tree in the wild is sometimes prolific, and seedlings are most easily obtained by harvesting this crop.
Uses: *Z. davyi* is well worth growing for its form, its trunk, unique to its genus, and to attract birds. Fruits first appear at about six years. Growth rate is about 70 cm per year. *Z. davyi* likes a temperate or warm summer with good rainfall.

Ziziphus mucronata
Buffalo thorn

Size: 3–15 x 3–12 m (wild), up to 8 x 7 m (garden)
Natural habitat: *Ziziphus* is widespread, being absent only from the Karoo and fynbos. It occurs in most habitats, particularly in deciduous woodland.
Growth form: Shape varies, but it usually has rugged twists or forks in the trunk. The branches are very spiny. The leaves are glossy and flush a delicate pale green in spring. A good crop of red-brown berries is produced every year. They stay on the tree, in edible condition, for months. Birds, especially bulbuls and louries, like them, and fallen fruits are pounced upon by mammals. *Ziziphus* is the host of the butterflies *Tarucus sybaris* and several species of *Castalius*.
Propagation: Seed.
Uses: *Ziziphus* makes an excellent barrier plant and adequate shade tree. It is a great provider for animals, a tree of life. Flowering and fruiting begin at four years. *Ziziphus* attracts warblers, robins and shrikes, because of the wealth of insects that it supports. Growth rate is about 1 m per year. It enjoys any climate except a cool wet one, so is especially useful in inhospitable gardens that support little else.

Make your own indigenous drinks Dare to be different. Distil your own delicious alcoholic drinks from the fruits of maroela (*Sclerocarya birrea*), or soak half-crushed green knobwood (*Zanthoxylum capense* or *davyi*) fruits in cane spirit, to make a fiery lemon gin.

INDEX

A
Acacia burkei **10**, 33, 103
Acacia caffra **10**, 33, 103
Acacia galpinii **11**, 33, 103
Acacia karroo **11**, 33, 87, 103
Acacia nigrescens 4, **12**, 33, 62, 103
Acacia nilotica **12**, 33, 103
Acacia robusta **13**, 33, 103
Acacia sieberiana **13**, 33, 103
Acacia tortilis **14**, 33, 103
Acacia xanthophloea **14**, 33, 62, 103
Adansonia digitata **15**
African dog-rose 107
African mangosteen 58
African mulberry 71
African teak 21
Albizia adianthifolia **15**, 87
Androstachys johnsonii **16**
Antidesma venosum **16**
Apodytes dimidiata **17**
assegai tree 38
Atalaya alata **17**

B
Balanites maughamii **18**
baobab 15
Baphia racemosa **18**
Barringtonia racemosa **19**
basterperdepis 63
bats 8
bean tree 69
bergboegoe 36
berg cypress 106
Bersama lucens **19**
big ears 103
birds 7–8, 24, 35, 47, 54, 70, 78, 101
bitter almond 82
bitter-leaf 21
black monkey-thorn 10
blue guarri 48
boekenhout 52
Bolusanthus speciosus **20**, 25
bonsai 10, 12, 14, 34, 54, 56, 62, 73, 94, 106
borer beetle 96
bostaaibos 86
bosvlier 72
Brachylaena discolor **20**
Brachylaena elliptica **21**
Breonadia microcephala **21**
Bridelia micrantha **22**
brittle wood 72
broad-leaved coral tree 47
broad-leaved resin tree 75
bronze paper commiphora 33
Buddleja saligna **22**
Buddleja salviifolia **23**
buffalo thorn 109
bush guarri 49
butterflies 8

C
cabbage tree 40
Calodendrum capense **23**
Calpurnia aurea **24**
Camdeboo stinkwood 27
camphor bush 99
candlewood 89
Canthium mundianum **24**, 62
Cape ash 45
Cape beech 84
Cape chestnut 23
Cape fig 55
Cape holly 64
Cape laurel 37
Cape plane 73
Cape teak 96
carrot tree 94
Cassia abbreviata **25**
Cassia petersiana 6, **25**
Cassine aethiopica **26**
Cassine transvaalensis **26**
Celtis africana **27**, 56, 87
Celtis mildbraedii **27**
Chaetacme aristata **28**
Chaka's wood 96
chemicals 7, 20, 79
cherrywood 84
Chrysophyllum viridifolium **28**
Cladostemon kirkii 6, **29**

Clerodendrum glabrum **29**
coast goldleaf 22
coast silverleaf 20
Cola greenwayi **30**
Colophospermum mopane **30**
Combretum erythrophyllum **31**
Combretum imberbe **31**
Combretum kraussii **32**
Combretum molle **32**
Combretum zeyheri **33**
Commiphora harveyi 6, **33**, 56
Commiphora neglecta 6, **34**, 56
Commiphora pyracanthoides 6, **34**, 56
Commiphora schimperi 6, **35**, 56
common coral tree 48
common hook-thorn 10
common spike-thorn 61
common star-chestnut 95
common taaibos 88
Cordia caffra **35**
craibia 36
Craibia zimmermannii **36**
cross-pollination 35
Croton gratissimus **36**
Croton sylvaticus **37**
Cryptocarya woodii **37**
Cunonia capensis **38**
Curtisia dentata **38**
Cussonia natalensis 33, **39**
Cussonia paniculata 33, **39**
Cussonia spicata 33, **40**
cuttings 6
Cyathea dregei **40**

D
Dais cotinifolia **41**
Deinbollia oblongifolia **41**
Dichrostachys cinerea 15, **42**
Diospyros mespiliformis **42**
Diospyros natalensis **43**
dogplum 45
dogwood 86
Dombeya rotundifolia **43**
Dombeya tiliacea **44**
doppruim 76
Dovyalis longispina **44**, 92
Drypetes natalensis **45**
duiker-berry 90
dune forest 19
dune soap-berry 41
dwarf coral tree 47

E
Ekebergia capensis **45**
Englerophytum magalismontanum **46**
Englerophytum natalense **46**
enkeldoring 13
Erythrina humeana 25, **47**, 48
Erythrina latissima 25, **47**, 48
Erythrina lysistemon 25, **48**
essenhout 45
Euclea crispa **48**
Euclea natalensis **49**
Euclea racemosa **49**
Euclea schimperi see Euclea racemosa
Eugenia umtamvunensis **50**
Eugenia zuluensis **50**
Euphorbia cooperi **51**
Euphorbia ingens **51**

F
false soap-berry 76
Faurea saligna **52**
fertiliser 105
fever tree 14
Ficus abutilifolia 33, **52**, 56
Ficus capensis see Ficus sur
Ficus glumosa 33, **53**, 56
Ficus hippopotami see Ficus trichopoda
Ficus ingens 33, **53**, 56
Ficus lutea 33, **54**, 56
Ficus natalensis 33, **54**, 56
Ficus sansibarica 33, **55**, 56
Ficus soldanella see Ficus abutilifolia
Ficus sonderi see Ficus glumosa
Ficus sur 33, **55**, 56
Ficus sycomorus 33, **56**
Ficus tremula 33, **56**
Ficus trichopoda 33, **57**, 56
Ficus vogelii see Ficus lutea

fire thorn 88
flatcrown 15
flower colours 38, 43, 58, 91, 95
fluted milkwood 28
forest 16
forest bushwillow 32
forest croton 37
forest dombeya 44
forest toad tree 98
frost 4, 6, 17, 76, 83

G
Galpinia transvaalica 4, 49, **57**
Garcinia livingstonei 44, **58**
garden design 4–5
Gardenia spatulifolia see Gardenia volkensii
Gardenia thunbergia **58**
Gardenia volkensii **59**
germination see seeds
giant-leaved fig 54
giant raisin 60
glossy bersama 19
glossy-leaved commiphora 35
Gonioma kamassi **59**
green-apple 70
green flower tree 77
green witch-hazel 102
Grewia hexamita **60**
Greyia sutherlandii 47, **60**
Gymnosporia buxifolia **61**

H
hairy cola 30
Halleria lucida 25, 47, **61**
hardekool 31
Henkel's yellowwood 80
Heteromorpha arborescens
    see Heteromorpha trifoliata
Heteromorpha trifoliata **62**
Heteropyxis natalensis **62**
Hippobromus pauciflorus **63**
hippo fig 57
huilboom 78
Hymenocardia ulmoides **63**
Hyphaene coriacea **64**

I
ilala palm 64
Ilex mitis **64**
indigenous gardening 4, 72
ingwavuma 26
inhambanella 65
Inhambanella henriquesii **65**
insects 7, 37

J
jackal-berry 42
jakkalsbessie 42
jams 92

K
kamassi 59
kanniedood 34
karee 87
kasuur 79
kershout 84
keurboom 105
kiepersol 40
Kigelia africana **65**
Kiggelaria africana **66**
Kirkia acuminata **66**
klipels 24
knob thorn 12
knobwood 109
kooboo berry 26
Kosi palm 85

L
Lagynias lasiantha **67**
large-fruited bushwillow 33
large-leaved bride's bush 77
large-leaved guarri 49
large-leaved rock fig 52
large sourplum 107
lavender croton 36
lavender tree 62
layering 61
leadwood 31
leaves
    colour 31, 55, 81
    scent 99

GLOSSARY

Aril: an edible growth, attached to a seed
Asymmetrical: not symmetric; unevenly divided
Basal cup: cup in which the base of a fruit sits
Catkin: a crowded spike of very small flowers
Cell sap: fluid in the plant cells
Compound leaf: a leaf divided into separate leaflets
Dominant: most common species in a habitat, sometimes outnumbering all others combined
Eco-mates: species sharing the same micro-habitat
Epiphytic: rooted in leaf litter in tree forks: not parasitic
Layered branches: horizontal branches arranged in neat, clearly separated layers
Leaflet: a division of a compound leaf
Localised endemic: a species of very restricted natural range
Locally abundant or common: common in some parts of their natural range
Locally dominant: dominant in some parts of their natural range
Massed show: flowers or fruits produced in sufficient abundance to produce a generous display
Multi-stemmed: having a trunk dividing at or below ground level
Mulch: a permeable material such as compost, dead leaves, humus, well rotted manure or small stones used to cover the soil to reduce evaporation
Native range: the geographical area in which a species grows naturally
Nursery mix: a mixture of soil, sand, compost, pine bark, or any other materials used for germinating or growing plants in nurseries
Palmately compound: a leaf divided radially from a single point into four or more leaflets
Petiole: a leaf stalk
Pinnate: a long compound leaf divided into a series of pairs of leaflets
Raceme: a sequence of flowers produced, one after another, up the same vertical stalk
Riverine thicket: dense vegetation lining river banks
Scramble: lean, sprawl or otherwise grow over surrounding vegetation
Secondary coloniser: a plant that grows only after other plants have first colonised new ground
Sepals: the ring of flower parts below and surrounding the petals
Single-species stand: a tree community consisting of just one species
Specimen: a tree of a species with an elegant profile, good-looking enough to be planted as an individual feature
Stamen: pollen-producing part of a flower
Stand: grove, small community
Stilt roots: roots put out, above ground, from the trunk, that later root in the soil
Stipule: a structure initially covering an emerging leaf
Style: a female component of a flower
Suckering: the sprouting of new stems from a damaged root
Trifoliolate: a leaf divided into three leaflets
Underbark: the layer of bark between the outer, rough bark layer and the trunk
Understorey: the smaller trees living in permanent shade in a forest, under the main tree canopy

SYMBOLS

- Grows best in full sun
- Grows best in partial shade
- Grows best in shade
- Deciduous tree (loses its leaves)
- Evergreen tree (never loses its leaves)
- Flowers are an attractive feature
- Fruit is an attractive feature
- Attracts butterflies
- Attracts birds
- Attracts bats
- Grows well in clay
- Survives severe drought
- Survives moderate drought
- Grows well in coastal sand and withstands coastal wind
- Grows in waterlogged soil
- Survives harsh frost
- Survives moderate frost
- Survives light frost

No frost symbol: Cannot survive frost

- Grows best in area with high rainfall
- Grows best in area with moderate rainfall
- Grows best in area with low rainfall

Lebombo cluster-leaf 99
Lebombo ironwood 16
Lebombo wing-nut 17
lekkerruikpeul 12
lemonwood 108
lesser candelabra tree 51
Leucosidea sericea **67**
long-tail cassia 25
Lowveld chestnut 95
Lowveld cluster-leaf 100
Lowveld tree vernonia 105
Loxostylis alata **68**

M
Macaranga capensis **68**
Markhamia acuminata
  see Markhamia zanzibarica
Markhamia zanzibarica **69**
maroela 92
matumi 21
Millettia grandis **69**
Mimusops obovata **70**
mingerhout 21
mitzeerie 22
monkey pod 25
monkey thorn 11
Monodora junodii **70**
mopane 30
Morus mesozygia **71**
mountain cabbage tree 39
mountain cedar 106
mountain karee 87
mountain olinia 74
mountain rock fig 53
myrtle bushwillow 83

N
naboom 51
Natal bottlebrush 60
Natal camwood 18
Natal dovyalis 44
Natal drypetes 45
Natal fig 54
Natal mahogany 102
Natal medlar 67
Natal milkplum 46
Natal white stinkwood 27
nitrogen (in acacias) 13
Noltea africana **71**
notsung 61
Nuxia congesta 7, **72**
Nuxia floribunda 7, **72**

O
Ochna arborea 4, **73**
Olea africana see Olea europaea
Olea europaea 56, **73**
Olinia emarginata **74**
Oncoba spinosa **74**
orchid tree 70
ouhout 67
Outeniqua yellowwood 79
Ozoroa engleri **75**
Ozoroa obovata **75**

P
Pancovia golungensis **76**
paperbark thorn 13
Pappea capensis **76**
parsley tree 62
parsnip tree 62
Pavetta edentula **77**
Peddiea africana **77**
Peddiea fischeri see Peddiea africana
Peltophorum africanum 25, **78**
pendoring 61
Phoenix reclinata **78**
pigeonwood 101
Pittosporum viridiflorum **79**
planting 6–7
Podocarpus falcatus 5, **79**
Podocarpus henkelii 5, **80**
Podocarpus latifolius 5, **80**
pompon tree 41
Pondo myrtle 50
powderpuff tree 19
propagation
  cuttings 6
  layering 6
  seeds 5–6, 29, 30, 36
Protea roupelliae **81**
Protorhus longifolia **81**
pruning 7, 42, 93
Prunus africana **82**
Ptaeroxylon obliquum **82**

Pteleopsis myrtifolia **83**
Pterocarpus rotundifolius **83**
Pterocelastrus tricuspidatus **84**

Q
quinine tree 85
quiver-leaf fig 56

R
raasblaar 33
Rapanea melanophloeos **84**
Raphia australis **85**
Rauvolfia caffra **85**
real yellowwood 80
red beech 81
redcurrant 86
red heart 63
red-leaved rock fig 53
red milkwood 70
red pear 92
red stinkwood 82
Rhamnus prinoides 49, **86**
Rhus chirindensis **86**
Rhus lancea **87**
Rhus leptodictya **87**
Rhus pallens **88**
Rhus pyroides **88**
Rinorea angustifolia 49, **89**
river bushwilllow 31
riverine forest 74
rock alder 24
rooiels 38
Rothmannia capensis 25, **89**
Rothmannia globosa 25, **90**
round-leaf kiaat 83

S
saddle pod 106
saffronwood 26
sagewood 23
sand forest 18
Sapium integerrimum **90**
sausage tree 65
scented thorn 12
Schotia brachypetala 25, 47, **91**
Schrebera alata **91**
Sclerocarya birrea **92**, 109
Scolopia mundii **92**
Securidaca longipedunculata **93**
seedlings, wild 28, 98
seeds
  abrasion 5
  fire treatment 5, 36
  germination 5, 30, 103
  planting 5
  storing 5, 29
sekelbos 42
septee 35
September bells 90
sickle bush 42
Sideroxylon inerme **93**
silver protea 81
simple-leaved cabbage tree 39
sjambok pod 25
small knobwood 108
small-leaved jackal-berry 43
sneezewood 82
snuffbox tree 74
soap dogwood 71
spiny monkey-orange 96
Spirostachys africana 62, **94**
splendid acacia 13
stamvrug 46
Steganotaenia araliacea **94**
Sterculia murex **95**
Sterculia rogersii **95**
Strychnos decussata **96**
Strychnos spinosa **96**
Suregada zanzibariensis **97**
swamp fig 57
swamp forest 19, 22
sweet-root commiphora 34
sweet thorn 11
sycamore fig 56
Syzygium cordatum **97**

T
Tabernaemontana elegans 25, **98**
Tabernaemontana ventricosa 25, **98**
tamboti 94
Tarchonanthus camphoratus 99
tassel berry 16
Terminalia phanerophlebia 99
Terminalia prunioides **100**
Terminalia sericea 100

termites 64
Thespesia acutiloba **101**
thornveld trees 12
thorny elm 28
three-finger bush 29
tierhout 68
toad tree 98
torchwood 18
Toxicodendron succedanea 88
Transvaal gardenia 59
tree fern 40
tree fuchsia 61
tree wistaria 20
Trema orientalis **101**
Trichilia emetica 87, **102**
Trichocladus grandiflorus **102**
Trimeria grandifolia **103**
Turraea floribunda 66, **103**

U
umbrella thorn 14
umdoni 97
umkhuhlu 102
umzimbeet 69

V
vaalboom 100
vaalbos 99
Vangueria infausta **104**
vanwykshout 20
velvet bushwillow 32
Vepris lanceolata **104**
Vepris undulata see Vepris lanceolata
verbena tree 29
Vernonia colorata **105**
violet pea 18
violet tree 93
Virgilia divaricata **105**
vlier 72

W
warty taaibos 88
watering 26, 85
weeping boer-bean 91
weeping wattle 78
white cat's whiskers 29
white gardenia 58
white ironwood 104
white milkwood 93
white pear 17
white resin tree 75
white stinkwood 27
white syringa 66
white violet-bush 89
Widdringtonia nodiflora **106**
wild date palm 78
wildevlier 72
wild honeysuckle tree 103
wild jasmine 91
wild laburnum 24
wild medlar 104
wild myrtle 50
wild olive 73
wild peach 66
wild pear 43
wild poplar 68
wild pride-of-India 57
wild silver oak 20
wild tulip tree 101
wind 4., 23
witolienhout 22
woodland suregada 97
woodland trees 10
Wrightia natalensis **106**

X
Ximenia caffra 44, 92, **107**
Xylotheca kraussiana **107**
Xymalos monospora **108**

Z
Zanthoxylum capense **108**, 109
Zanthoxylum davyi **109**
Zanzibar fig 55
Ziziphus mucronata 7, 86, **109**